The Best of Jim Davidson

The
BEST
of Jim
Davidson

**Most Requested Selections
From The Author's Nationally
Syndicated Radio Series**

Jim Davidson

Strategic Book Publishing and Rights Co.

Strategic Book Publishing and Rights Co., LLC
USA | Singapore
www.sbpra.net

For information about special discounts for bulk purchases, please contact Strategic Book Publishing and Rights Co. Special Sales, at bookorder@sbpra.net.

ISBN: 978-1-950015-64-1

Book Design: Suzanne Kelly

Acknowledgements

It is with my heartfelt thanks and gratitude that I acknowledge the hundreds of people whose names appear in the following pages and also the many unnamed individuals who have contributed to the publication of this book in one way or another. I also wish to thank our many *How to Plan Your Life* radio sponsors, because without them our program could not be on the air, along with stations that carry our program and the millions of listeners, many of whom have expressed their love and appreciation.

I would be remiss if I did not pay tribute to the late Earl Nightingale, because it was his motivational programs on cassette that provided the inspiration and encouragement that led me to begin a new career. Earl was known as the Dean of Personal Motivation. His daily radio program "Our Changing World" was carried by over 1,000 stations, making it the largest commercially sponsored program in the history of broadcasting. For several years it was my honor to represent him, and sell his motivational recordings in the state of Arkansas.

My car, with a cassette player installed, became a "classroom on wheels" as I listened to Earl's recorded messages repetitively, while driving over 50,000 miles each year. Truly he had collected the wisdom of the ages, and this knowledge was embedded deeply in my subconscious mind. When you read this book that you hold in your hands, I believe you will agree that his words fell on fertile soil and I feel so blessed to be able to pass along these ideas and concepts to you. Without the publication of this book, many of these life-changing ideas would be lost. Oh, I also became an avid reader and now have a fine home library.

I would also like to pay tribute to my mentor, the late Winston K. Pendleton, of Windermere, Florida, who took me under his wing and helped me in so many ways. Last, but by no means least, my special thanks to Dave McCree, our broadcast director, who has done a fine job of narrating the program for our company.

This book is dedicated to my wife Janis.
She is the joy and love of my life.

Introduction

In 1979, I began a daily radio program titled *"How to Plan Your Life"* and it has now been carried by over 300 stations coast-to-coast and heard by thousands of people each day. This book is a collection of sixty of my most requested individual programs, and they cover a wide range of topics and subject matter. But most of all it is a book of hope, encouragement and inspiration that is meant to lift your spirits and renew your faith in God and your fellow human beings.

As you read along, it will help you to know that each program only requires about three minutes of radio air time and each one is more or less self-contained. This is to say that each program begins with some opening or introductory comments, followed by a central theme or idea and is then summarized with a personal benefit for you. In most cases the benefit will be obvious, but in others you will have to dwell on the central theme or idea before it will become clear.

If you will think about it a moment, I believe you will agree that this format has several advantages. Unlike most books that have a story line that begins in chapter one and continues to the end of the book, here you can get the full impact or benefit in only a few minutes of reading time. This is especially helpful for those people who love to read but are so busy they don't make the time for a regular reading program. On somewhat of a humorous note, I am told this book is a great "bathroom" book.

While this book was never meant to be a success motivation or positive thinking book, it could turn out to be all of that and more for you. While success is a relative thing and it's very personal, it is also one of the most important intrinsic attributes we have going for us as human beings. To some degree, all human beings want to be successful in life, regardless of what our goals happen to be or what we set out to accomplish. In the beginning at least, no person wants to fail or be miserable in life. In far too many cases, however, it turns out this way. Our overcrowded prisons and bulging welfare rolls serve as constant reminder of this fact.

While I don't make any claim to the ideas in this book being original with me, they are the very best I have been able to find in many, many years of reading and research. Here is how I believe you can best use these ideas to your advantage. After you finish reading this introduction, take a few minutes and scan the Subject Index in the back of the book. Here you will find topics that address most any area of life where you have an opportunity or a challenge. You can then take these ideas and use them for specific guidelines to solve a problem or use them as a source of encouragement and inspiration to get back up during those low times we all experience. You can also use them to help others.

You will find programs that are humorous, like "Hit a Stroke and Drag Charlie" and "I Bet There Ain't No $12.00 Sewing Machine Either!" along with programs that are sad, like "The Silent Patients Speak" and "Should You Go First." Then there are other programs on rearing children, goal setting, education, marriage, and many, many more. My most requested program of all is titled, "The T.J. Miracle Diet", and it can be found on page 223. Believe me, this diet works!

In addition to your own personal needs, there may be other ways these ideas can be put to good use. Some time back, a man in Foley, Alabama, told me he uses one of these programs to begin their Rotary Club program each week. A school secretary reports that she uses many of the positive quotes and poems in their monthly school newsletter. Then, too, many people have said, "I hope you don't mind, but I used one of the stories in your book in a speech I made the other day."

My answer to them is the same one I would give to you. "Use these programs and ideas in any way you can, that will help you or others. That's what they are here for." My prayer is that you will use these ideas and concepts to be of greater service to your fellow human beings. This is the best way on earth to live.

Jim Davidson
Conway, Arkansas

Table of Contents

Training

Do You Have Class?

*In today's times, the person we consider to
have "class" is just someone with good
manners. Mark Twain once said, "Training
is everything. The peach was once a bitter
almond; cauliflower is nothing but a
cabbage with a college education."*

Sometime ago, my wife and I attended a
graduation exercise for a class of nurses at a local
hospital. Near the end of the program, the head
instructor read an article titled, "What is Class?" It
was so interesting, I went to her after the exercise
and asked for a copy. I want to share it with you.

1

We often hear it said of another that he or she has class, but have you ever thought about what the word *class* really means when it's used in reference to an individual? The word, used in this context, is entirely different than my earlier reference to a class of nurses. As you read this article about class, think about it as it relates to your life.

Class

Class never runs scared. It is sure-footed and confident that you can meet life head-on and handle whatever comes along.

Class never makes excuses. It takes its lumps and learns from past mistakes.

Class is considerate of others. It knows that good manners are nothing more than a series of petty sacrifices.

Class bespeaks an aristocracy that has nothing to do with ancestors or money. The most affluent blueblood can be totally without class, while the descendant of a Welsh miner may ooze class from every pore.

Class never tries to build itself up by tearing others down. Class is already up; it cannot look better by making others look worse.

Class can walk with kings and keep its virtue and talk with crowds and keep the common touch. Everyone is comfortable with the person who has class, because he is comfortable with himself.

If you don't have it, no matter what else you have, it doesn't make much difference.

To me, this article is as rich as a malt with four eggs for a thinking person. I especially like the thought, "class never makes excuses; it takes its lumps and learns from past mistakes." Wouldn't we all be better off if we could learn to do that?

I know many times when I have failed to do something, I usually try to find a way to justify my actions. Then I say, "I did it because..." In some cases, I've said to myself, "I wouldn't have done that if it hadn't been for so-and-so." All I was doing was trying to transfer the blame for my own failure to someone else.

I think we should never be too hard on ourselves, because if we do that on a regular basis, we are putting ourselves down, and the result will surely be low self-esteem. We do, however, need high standards because it's the only way to improve. For example, where would pole vaulters be if they didn't have someone to raise the bar?

When it comes to personal accountability and establishing a standard for personal behavior,

I don't believe you can improve on the qualities mentioned in the article on class. Ask yourself, "do I have class?" If you don't, would you like to have it? Of course, it takes much more than just saying it to make it so, but the first step is to start acting like a person who has class. Who knows? It may become a wonderful habit.

The Hall of Fame and Who's Who contain few portraits of men and women who were content with things as they were.

Unknown

Four Marks of an Educated Person

*Regardless of the flag it may be flying,
the ship of education will take you more
places, faster and with greater comfort than
any other ship on earth. The irony of this
statement is that it has not always been true.*

Some time ago, there was an article by Grayson Kirk in The Rotarian entitled, "The Four Marks of an Educated Person." As my close friends and those who listen to my daily radio program know, I am a strong believer in the merits of a good education. I felt so strongly about this when we organized our company, we named it Continuing

5

Education Services. From my perspective, the word "continuing" is the key. We sometimes fail to realize that our real education begins after we leave school.

Let me ask you a related question: Did you hear about the fellow who had a B.A., an M.A., and a Ph.D., but he didn't have a J.O.B.?

As you think about your own life and where you are now, I would like to pass along Mr. Kirk's thoughts from his article, "The Four Marks of An Educated Person," and see if you don't also agree with him.

No. 1 The educated person speaks and writes clearly and precisely, no matter how much information he may have stored away in his brain. A person is not educated until he learns to use his mother tongue with grace, precision and clarity.

No. 2 The educated person has a set of values and the courage to defend them. Knowledge and experience have given him the capacity to discriminate not only between right and wrong, but also between the trivial and the significant, between that which is cheap and that which has integrity.

No. 3 The educated person tries to understand his society and how it differs from others. He views these differences with compassion and respect, where the uneducated man sees them as evidence of his own superiority, regarding the customs of others with condemnation or contempt.

No. 4 The educated person looks squarely at the world and all of its problems, but always with hope. He neither fears nor rejects the trials and tribulations of modern life, but accepts as his responsibility the task of making order out of complexity and opportunity out of danger.

There are always exceptions to the rule, but I can't think of many people whom I consider to be educated who do not possess these qualities. Can you? There is a lot of food for thought in this article. Give yourself a check up from time to time. That's what I plan to do!

> *Learn to know yourself to the end that you may improve your powers, your conduct, your character. This is the same aim of education and the best of all education is self-education.*
> Rutherford B. Hayes

A Sound Philosophy in Ten Sentences

When it comes to philosophy, most people would rather skip class, because the subject is often perceived as something vague and abstract. In reality, our personal philosophy determines our attitudes, values, and the way we view the world and the people around us. As Oliver Braston once said, "Philosophy is just common sense in a dress suit."

A United States Senator was visiting a small town in his home state, and he stopped to visit one of the locals who was sitting on a bench at the court house. During the conversa-

8

tion he asked the man, "What's your political philosophy?"

After thinking a moment, the man said, "Well, I'll tell you Senator, my political philosophy is that we ought to take all the money, all the real estate, all the stocks and bonds and anything else of value and divide it up equal between every man, woman and child in the country." He said, "That's my philosophy, and I think it would be fair."

At this point, the Senator took the time to explain that the man's idea was not original. He went on to say, "If this were to come to pass, it would be less than a generation before those people who worked a little harder, stayed up a little later, and provided more service to their fellow man, would earn it all back." He concluded his comments by saying, "The wealth would be back in the hands of those who earned it, and the lazy and the ne'er-do-well would lose theirs."

After the man heard him out, he said, "Senator, you have missed the point completely; I mean divide it up equal *every* Saturday."

While this is just a story, it is not as far-fetched as it might seem on the surface. In fact, a lot of people in America view our economic prosperity this way. In truth, we hope this never happens. When political events and economic trends in our country kill the incentive for our citizens to get ahead, they will have effectively killed the greatest economic system the world has ever devised.

Now, may I pose this question to you? What is your philosophy of life? Have you ever thought about it? I'm sure some people have, but on the other hand, I'm confident that millions of people in our great nation have never given much thought to their own personal philosophy of life. Some time ago, I discovered something in my files titled "A Sound Philosophy in Ten Sentences," and I would like to share it with you. After you finish reading it, see what you think of these ideas.

1. You cannot lift the wages of the wage earner by pulling down the wage payer.

2. You cannot bring about prosperity by discouraging thrift.

3. You cannot keep out of trouble by spending more than your income.

4. You cannot establish sound currency on borrowed money.

5. You cannot help the poor by destroying the rich.

6. You cannot build character and courage by taking away initiative.

7. You cannot strengthen the weak by weakening the strong.

8. You cannot further humanity by inciting class hatred.

9. You cannot help small people by tearing down big people.

10. You cannot really help men and women by having their government tax them, to do for them the things they should do for themselves.

Anonymous

Could you add parts of this "Sound Philosophy in Ten Sentences" to your own? Could this benefit you in some way?

Every man who rises above the common level has received two educations: the first from his teachers, the second, more personal and important, from himself.
Edward Gibbon

Philosophy is the discovery of what is true, and the practice of that which is good.
Voltaire

Children

How to Raise a Crook

With the "good life" that people have in prison these days, there should be some type of course taught that would help to prepare those who have an interest to get it. Hopefully, you realize I've just made a facetious statement. No self-respecting person wants to wind up in prison and certainly parents who love their children do not want to see them go wrong and find themselves tucked away in some prison to spend a good part of their lives.

Quite to the contrary, those of us who love our children want the very best futures for them, and want them to become productive, responsible, law-abiding citizens. While this is just common sense, apparently a lot of people do not realize their own attitudes and behavior contribute to the real possibility of one or more of their children winding up in prison.

Have you ever said to yourself "If only?" "If only I hadn't married that man or that woman." "If only I had paid more attention to my teachers in school." "If only I'd have been more careful who I ran around with." "If only I had listened to what my parents were trying to teach me." Yes, when you really get serious about it, a lot of people go through life with their "if onlys."

Along these lines I want to share, "How to Raise a Crook," printed some time ago in *The Presbyterian Journal.* I hope if you are a parent or someone who is in a position to influence the values, morals, and character of young people, you may benefit from it. If you'll think about it, much of what we learn comes from the experience of others who have also said "if only."

If You Want to Raise a Crook:

1. Begin from infancy to give the child everything he wants: this way he will grow up to believe the world owes him a living.

2. When he picks up bad words, laugh at him—it will encourage him to pick up "cuter" phrases that will blow the top of your head off later.

3. Never give him spiritual training. Wait until he is twenty-one and then let him decide for himself.

4. Avoid the use of the word "wrong." He may develop a guilt complex. This will condition him to believe later, when he is arrested for stealing a car, that society is against him and that he is being persecuted.

5. Pick up anything he leaves lying around: books, shoes, clothing. Do everything for him so he will be experienced in throwing the responsibility onto others.

6. Let him read any printed matter he can get his hands on. Be careful the silverware and drinking glasses are sterilized, but let his mind feed on garbage.

7. Quarrel frequently in the presence of children, then they won't be too shocked when the home is broken up.

8. Give the child all the spending money he wants. Never let him earn his own. Why should he have things as tough as you had them?

9. Satisfy his every need for food, drink and comfort. Denial may lead to harmful frustrations.

10. Take his part against the neighbors, teachers and policemen. They are all prejudiced against your child.

11. When he gets into real trouble, apologize for yourself by saying "I never could do anything with him."

If you want to raise a crook, I believe these suggestions will help.

> *They who educate children well, are*
> *more to be honored than they who*
> *produce them; for these only gave them*
> *life, those the art of living well.*
>
> Aristotle

Excellence

The Touch of the Master's Hand

One time, I heard a very famous person make this statement: "In most any circumstance, if you will watch what the crowd is doing and do exactly the opposite, you'll probably never make another mistake as long as you live." You may recall the most famous trial in history ended when Pontius Pilate asked the crowd, "What shall I do with this man, Jesus?" and the crowd yelled, "Crucify him!" Yes, it was the crowd that sent Jesus to the cross.

As you ponder this thought, I would like you to consider this familiar poem.

The Touch of the Master's Hand

'Twas battered and scarred, and the auctioneer
Thought it scarcely worth his while
To waste much time on the old violin,
But he held it up with a smile;
"What am I bidden, good folk?" he cried,
   "Who'll start the bidding for me?
A dollar, one dollar; then two, only two;
Two dollars, and who'll make it three?
Going for three," but no!
From the room far back, a gray haired man
Came forward and picked up the bow;
Then wiping the dust from the old violin,
And tightening the loose strings,
He played a melody pure and sweet
As a caroling angel sings.
The music ceased and the auctioneer,
With a voice that was quiet and low,
Said, "Now what am I bid for the old violin?"
And he held it up with the bow;
"A thousand dollars, and who'll make it two?
Two thousand and who'll make it three?
Three thousand once, three thousand twice,
And going, and gone" cried he;
The people cheered, but some of them cried,
"We do not understand;
What changed it's worth?" Quick came the
   reply,

"The touch of the master's hand."
And many a man with life out of tune,
And battered and scarred with sin,
Is auctioned cheap to a thoughtless crowd,
Much like the old violin.
A mess of pottage, a glass of wine,
A game, and he travels on;
He's going once, and going twice! He's going,
    and almost gone!
But the Master comes, and the foolish crowd
Never can quite understand
The worth of a soul, and the change that's
    wrought
By the Touch of the Master's Hand.

                    Myra Brooks Welch

At some time in your life, if you have ever experienced the touch of the Master's hand, then you understand the message of this poem. Almost every day we pass people whose lives are 'out of tune' and yes, their lives are battered and scarred with sin. Sometimes, it's hard for those of us who make up the crowd to realize their lives can be made pure again by simply experiencing the touch of the Master's hand. Won't you allow God to use you to bring this illuminating truth to those who need hope where before there was none?

It takes no brains to be an atheist. Any stupid person can deny the existence of a supernatural power, because man's physical senses cannot detect it. But there cannot be ignored the influence of conscience, the respect we feel for moral law, the mystery of first life on what must have been a molten mass, or the marvelous order in which the universe moves us about on this earth. All of these evidence the handiwork of a beneficent deity. For my part, that deity is the God of the Bible and of Christ, His Son.

Dwight D. Eisenhower

Credibility

"I Bet There Ain't No Twelve Dollar Sewing Machine, Either!"

How many times do you have to catch another person in an outright lie, before you would begin to doubt everything else they say? The answer to that question is once, because from that point on there will always be an unmistakable breach in his or her credibility. Save for those rare occasions when the truth would cause another person great emotional pain or bodily harm, telling the truth is the only sure way to achieve a lasting and meaningful success.

Some time ago, I heard a humorous story I believe illustrates the importance of credibility. This is one of those stories I heard at deer camp, but the man who told it, told it for the truth.

In the early 1930s, when times were really hard in our country, a woman from a rural southeast Arkansas community was married to a man who was from near Trenton, Tennessee. This was during the Great Depression. Times were really tough for the couple in Tennessee and the woman's relatives in Arkansas learned of their condition.

As a result of the news, Babe Ogles, one of her uncles, took it upon himself to write the couple a letter. He painted a very optimistic picture. "Luther," he wrote, "we want you and Aire Mae to load up and come to Arkansas. We can raise a cotton crop together and there are plenty of wild hogs in the woods here, so we can have lots of fresh meat. In fact, prices in town are very reasonable. You can even get a new sewing machine for twelve dollars and prices on other things are reasonable, too."

When Luther got this letter, he thought he had died and gone to heaven! In fact, he couldn't wait to get loaded up and headed out. They traveled the better part of two days in an old Model A Ford and got to her uncle's house late at night. Naturally, they had to wake everybody. When they all got up and were sitting around talking, Luther said, "Uncle Babe, the first thing in the morning can we go out and get one of them wild hogs? Me and Aire Mae ain't had any fresh meat in months, and as soon as we get settled, I'll be ready to start that cotton crop."

At this point, Uncle Babe was on the spot, so he said, "Sure Luther, we'll go out first thing in the morning." After breakfast, Uncle Babe got his single shot, twenty-two rifle down from the gun rack and they headed out through the woods in the back of the house.

Before long, they came upon some hogs and Uncle Babe picked out a good one and took aim and fired. He was a crack shot and the hog fell almost in its tracks. He turned to Luther and said, "Here, hold this gun!" grabbed the hog, slung it over his shoulder and started running.

Luther said, "How come you're in such a hurry, Uncle Babe, we got us a wild hog, ain't we?" Uncle Babe said, "Yeah, but I don't think the folks who own this hog will understand." You see, Uncle Babe had shot someone else's hog! As they were running through the woods, Luther said to himself, "Humph! I bet there ain't no twelve dollar sewing machine either."

Would you say Uncle Babe lost his credibility with Luther?

The moral of this story is simple: if we want to have credibility with another person, we must always tell the truth. As I heard a famous speaker say one time, "There is no price too great to pay for credibility." If we don't tell the truth, whether it's in relation to our jobs, our families, our relationships with other people or any other area of life, we are building our own future on sand, and it will not stand.

And you shall know the truth, and the truth shall make you free.

John 8:32

All I know is, it is better to tell the truth than to lie, better to be free than a slave, better to have knowledge than to be ignorant.

H. L. Mencken

Friends

When You Get Involved with Drugs, You Never Know Who Your "Friends" Are

The late Thomas Hughes, English author and reformer, once said, "Blessed are they who have the gift of making friends, for it is one of God's best gifts. It involves many things, but above all, the power of going out of one's self, and appreciating whatever is noble and loving in another." This is certainly a true statement and one that those of us who cherish our friends can really appreciate.

However, there is a moral and social crisis in the world today which can make it difficult to know who our true friends really are. I'm referring to the terrible scourge of illegal drugs. For those who choose to get involved, the idea or thought of a true friendship can quite often be a rude and painful awakening. There are millions of tragic stories that will bear this out, and I have one of those stories to share with you.

This true story involves a young person who got involved with drugs and it took place only a few miles from where I live, so it really hit close to home.

This person, a young man in his twenties, was a college student. Like so many others, he fell into bad company and before long, he was using drugs on a regular basis.

During this time, he met another young man and they became friends. They began to spend quite a bit of time together. The young man my story is about had been left an old house in a will, and he was fixing it up to live in, and his friend even spent several days helping him get it ready.

A few miles from the college town where they were both living, they had started a marijuana field, to grow plants, harvest them, and sell the drug to other students, and anyone else who came along. One afternoon just a short time ago, they both left school early to go to the marijuana field to harvest some plants. It had become their custom for one of them to carry a gun, since they had become wary of the local authorities.

As they made their way through a thicket of small pine trees, the young man was a few feet in front of his friend. He heard the hammer of the gun click. The next thing he knew, he was lying on the ground dazed, presumed to be dead by his friend who shot him.

As he continued to lay there, he heard the bite of a shovel, as it tore hunks out of the pine floor. His friend was digging a grave. Realizing his only chance to survive was a knife he carried in his pocket, he slowly pulled it out and opened the blade. His real problem, however, was that the blast of the gun had left him blinded.

When his so-called friend, who had now become his assailant, finished digging and came over to put him in the grave, the young man, upon hearing footsteps close by, lunged at him with the open knife blade and it ripped into the calf of his assailant's leg. He expected to be finished off, but his assailant left without doing him further harm. Later, it was revealed he had left to go get medical attention.

For the next two days and nights, in a mosquito and snake infested forest, the young man wandered—totally blind—until he finally staggered upon a farm house where he was able to find help. Today he is living with his parents in a nearby town and he will be blind for the rest of his life.

While the subject of drugs and the havoc they wreak in people's lives is endless, I believe this true story will shed light on the problem from a little different angle. It's true, "When you get involved with drugs, you never know who your friends are."

Even in the common affairs of life, in love, friendship, and marriage, how little security have we when we trust our happiness in the hands of others.

William Hazlitt

Goals

Beginners Should Set Only One Goal at a Time

It is often said, "The person without a goal is like a ship without a rudder." If we were to simply untie a ship, give it no crew, no compass or destination, but just let it drift, if it got out of the harbor at all, it would most likely sink or wind up on some deserted beach. Contrast this with the ship that has a crew, a compass and a definite port in mind. The odds are about ninety-nine percent it will reach its destination. We know this is true, but we sometimes fail to realize that a ship can only reach one port at a time.

I would like to ask you to help me conduct a little experiment. Don't fudge by reading ahead, but how do you spell the word 'joke'? J-O-K-E, right? Now how do you spell 'folk'? F-O-L-K, right? Now, I must say, you have this spelling down pat, but how do you spell the white of an egg? If you said A-L-B-U-M-E-N, you would be right. But, if you said, Y-O-L-K, I'm sorry, I tricked you! The white of an egg is the albumen, the yellow is the yolk.

You might ask, "What is the purpose of this experiment?" It's to demonstrate a principle that has a great deal to do with a person achieving success. Once our minds are traveling in a given direction, it's very difficult to stop and change gears. We see this same principle in action while driving an automobile. When you go down the highway doing sixty miles per hour, you had better not put it in reverse, or you will be looking for a new transmission.

Let me share an idea that will help when you think about your direction in life. One reason we see so much confusion in people's lives is that they haven't been taught how to set goals, and as a result they have no direction and no aiming point. Sure, a lot of people have dreams, hopes and wishes, but they don't have specific, written goals. As a result, they spend a lot of unproductive time going from one thing to another, being tossed "to and fro," like that ship I mentioned earlier.

For a goal to be valid or worthy, it should be specific and not general; it should be realistic with a definite time limit; and it should be written down on paper. While working with thousands of people over the past twenty years, I have found that fully ninety-five percent of all people do not have their goals written down on paper. There are many reasons why this is important, the first being that it's a commitment (at least you have committed it to writing). This written form will allow you to review your goal often and with each repetition, drive it deeper and deeper into your subconscious mind.

If you happen to be a goal setter, you know how important this is, and you know how to go about it. If, however, you are a beginner in the business of goal setting, I want to make a very important suggestion. Beginners should set only one goal at a time. After the process becomes second nature and you have achieved enough success and the resources to diversify, more than one worthy goal is something many people can handle, but not in the very beginning. Most of the confusion in people's lives comes from trying to accomplish too many things at the same time.

After setting that one worthy goal important to you, blaze it in your memory, burn it into your mind. When you first wake up, think of that one goal. When you sit down to rest for a few minutes, think about that one goal. As you think about it and visualize it, the goal becomes crystallized and your focus will be sharp and clear.

Since we become what we think about, soon you will reach that goal. At this point, set another goal and set out again. You will find this simple process of setting only one goal at a time will take most of the confusion out of your life and will bring order and self-discipline. You will be happier and more contented, because you have something specific to work for, something to get out of bed for. Your self-image and your attitude will change for the better.

> *Get up when you fall down. We all fall down, but the biographies of those whom the world calls successful reveal that they get up when they fall down. Sometimes more than once they've had to pick themselves up and dust themselves off and keep on keeping on.*
>
> Paul Harvey

> *If you wish to reach the highest, begin at the lowest.*
>
> Publilius Syrus

Smile. It May Improve Your Health!

A wise friend once said to me, "If you meet a man who cannot smile, give him one of yours, because no one needs a smile so much as the one who has none left to give." I have never forgotten that bit of wise counsel.

Recently, I had an opportunity to talk with a fine young man about his future. The young man, Jon, has excellent character and is a very hard worker, but when I'm around, he always has a very serious demeanor, so I gave him the following advice. I told him to relax and to make a conscious effort to smile more. I might add, my advice is well-founded.

A group of scientists at the University of California at San Francisco found that various facial expressions have a direct effect on the nervous system. According to their research, a smile affects the heart rate, blood pressure and respiration. In experiments they conducted, subjects were not told how to feel, but merely to move specific facial muscles. When subjects moved muscles to form a smile, they registered no change in their nervous system. However, when they made a frown or scowl, their heart rates went up dramatically. On the other hand, facial expressions that reflected any of several negative emotions like anger, fear or sadness, were all accompanied by increases in heart rate.

Another scientist says when we are aroused by some unpleasant happening, a smile will bring us back to normal more quickly. As it relates to our health, this research is telling us that it pays to smile.

Improving our health is only one of the many reasons why the natural inclination to smile can make a real difference in our lives. We will also find it's much easier to make friends and to communicate successfully with other people when we smile. This in turn will give us an advantage when it comes to earning more and achieving success in our careers. After all, most of us are in the "people business."

If you do not find it's easy and natural to smile as you interact with others, and it's something you would like to do more, here is an idea that may help you.

First, it's important to understand that we are creatures of habit. If our demeanor is rather serious, we are not going to change much without making a conscious effort. We must take matters into our own hands and make a conscious effort to smile. In the beginning, we may even find it necessary to over-do it a bit, until it begins to feel natural. I'm sure you have seen a small tree that was bent over and you had the feeling that you would like to straighten it up. To do this, you have to bend it to the extreme in the opposite direction. You may have to form a new habit in the same way; a habit that will pay big dividends in the future.

If you will give this some thought and begin to observe other people, here is what you will discover. For the most part, the people in every vocation and profession who are the most successful are those who project the spirit and attitude of happiness. When it comes to happiness, the best way to tell if people are happy is to catch them on a regular basis with twinkles in their eyes or big smiles on their faces. It's a dead giveaway!

> *I love the man that can smile in trouble,*
> *that can gather strength from distress,*
> *and grow brave by reflection. 'Tis*
> *the business of little minds to shrink,*
> *but he whose heart is firm and whose*
> *conscience approves his conduct, will*
> *pursue his principles until death.*
>
> Thomas Paine

> *A smile is a light in your window that*
> *lets other people know that someone is*
> *home.*
>
> Dennis Waitley

> *A joyful heart is good medicine, but a*
> *broken spirit dries up the bones.*
>
> Proverbs 17:22

Words of Wisdom from "Honest Abe"

*It has been said, "Wisdom is knowing
what to do next." Isn't this true? In every
situation in life, if we knew the right course
to take or the best decision to make, would
we not indeed be wise? In my own life, I
have found the best teacher is experience.
Not just my experience, but the experience
of others, too.*

I want to share a quotation by former President Abraham Lincoln that contains much wisdom.
He said: "Prosperity is the fruit of labor. Property
is desirable. It is a positive good in the world. That

some should be rich shows that others may become rich and hence is just encouragement to industry and enterprise. Let not him who is houseless pull down the house of another, but let him work diligently and build one for himself, thus by example assuring that his own shall be safe from violence when built."

These words were spoken by President Lincoln on March 21, 1864, and have been printed for distribution by the Will Rogers Rotary Club of Tulsa, Oklahoma. This quotation was sent to me by a radio listener and I was pleased to receive it, as I have had the opportunity to visit Ford's Theater in Washington, D.C., and Lincoln's restored home and his tomb in Springfield, Illinois. Today Lincoln is considered by many to be the greatest American President. The dark days of the Civil War only served to enhance and highlight the true character and fiber of this man.

Now you may ask, what makes a president, or any leader for that matter, really great? In many respects, people are much like metal; to know for sure what they are made of, they have to be tested. In the case of our nation's presidents, some served during a period of history when our nation was faced with great adversity and challenge. The events leading up to and during the Civil War certainly gave Abraham Lincoln an opportunity to prove what kind of man he was. It is often said, success is what happens when preparation meets opportunity.

The point I'm making here is simple and straightforward. In our country today, we need people like Abraham Lincoln in all walks of life who possess the character, commitment, honesty, insights, purpose and a true perspective of the really important things in life. In every community throughout this land, we need more men and women who cannot be bought, who won't sell out, and who truly understand what Abraham Lincoln stood for.

Take a moment and go back to the beginning of this chapter. Reread the quotation by Abraham Lincoln and give it some serious thought. I believe you will see the basis for much of the success that the United States of America enjoys today: physical labor, the importance of property, the opportunity to achieve financial success and the incentive for the individual and for business and industry to succeed.

His admonishment to the American people to "Let not him who is houseless pull down the house of another, but let him work diligently and build one for himself, thus by example assuring that his own shall be safe from violence when built" is the key. We must constantly strive to maintain the opportunity for all Americans to build and to foster character values and integrity, especially in our nation's youth so they will want to defend and preserve our way of life.

> *The prosperity of a country depends, not*
> *on the abundance of its revenues, nor*
> *on the strength of its fortifications, nor*
> *on the beauty of its public buildings, but*
> *it consists in the number of its men of*
> *enlightenment and character.*
>
> Martin Luther

Ineptitude

Addled Ads

*In the Bible, the prophet Isaiah certainly
did not have our nation's newspapers in
mind when he said in 52:7—"How beautiful
upon the mountains are the feet of him that
bringeth good tidings."*

In modern times, it's been proven over and
over again that good news is not what sells, it's the
bad news that drives millions to the newsstands
to purchase newspapers, even before the ink is
dry. While newspapers are in business to make a
profit (like any other American enterprise), most
of their revenue comes from advertising rather than
circulation.

Along this line, I ran across something a while back that was somewhat humorous and I would like to share it with you. Before doing so, this question please: Have you ever placed an ad in a newspaper, and when the paper came out, your ad was so fouled up you were unable to recognize it? Now, the newspaper people do a fine job, and I hope they won't mind if I poke a little good-natured fun at them here.

I ran across an article titled, "Addled Ads," from the collection of the National Composition Association. These are the folks who set type for the newspapers across the country. The article started off this way:

"For sale: a used sewing machine. Call Mr. Tom Kelly at 555-3455 after seven o'clock and ask for Mrs. Perkins who lives with him cheap."

The next day, there was a correction in the paper for this ad: "Correction: an error appeared in Mr. Tom Kelly's advertisement yesterday. It should have read: For sale, a used sewing machine cheap. Call Mr. Tom Kelly at 555-3455, and ask for Mrs. Perkins, who lives with him after seven o'clock."

The next day there was another correction: "Mr. Tom Kelly has reported several annoying telephone calls as a result of a classified advertisement that appeared in this newspaper yesterday. The ad stands corrected. For sale, a used sewing machine cheap. Call Mr. Tom Kelly after seven o'clock at 555-3455, and ask for Mrs. Perkins who loves with him."

The next day the paper carried the following notice. "I, Tom Kelly, no longer have a used sewing machine for sale. I took an ax and smashed it. I also no longer have a housekeeper. Mrs. Perkins resigned yesterday."

Even though the story is amusing, there are some things we might consider. When we see something like this, it's usually funny, unless of course, we happen to be the one who placed the ad, then it's not funny at all. In fact, when we are paying good money for something, we want it right.

The moral of this story is simple: So long as we are doing anything at all, we are bound to make some mistakes because that's the way we are. The fact is, the only people who don't make mistakes are in the cemetery. We should be very conscientious in our work, and do our best to do it right, whatever our work happens to be. We need to realize that even though it's just a job to us, the product or service we are providing to others is important.

In a free market economy, when people spend money, they have a right to receive something of value. When we give less than our best, we are eroding the very foundation of our nation's future. There is no way to build a sound product, economy or standard of living, unless we build in quality and value for the consumer. The next time you see an "addled ad," you can feel sorry for the customer, the newspaper, the typesetter and also for yourself, because in the long run, we all pay.

A man's ability cannot possibly be of one
sort and his soul another. If his soul be
well-ordered, serious, and restrained,
his ability is also sound and sober.
Conversely, when the one is degenerated
the other is contaminated.

Seneca

Written with Prejudice

The English critic and essayist, William Hazlitt (1778-1830), once said, "Prejudice is the child of ignorance." Without question prejudice has no place in a civilized society, because it leads to attitudes and actions based on conclusions that are preconceived, rather than information that is factual. Prejudice is usually associated with bigotry and hatred, but prejudice in itself is not necessarily bad. It can be good, if we are prejudiced toward the right things and in the right way. The real danger is that we often let our emotions get in the way.

Some time ago, Mr. Robert C. Howe, principal of the North Kansas City High School, was in Little Rock to address a conference of school administrators and I had the privilege of being in the audience. During his speech he shared something he called, "Written with Prejudice," and I enjoyed it so much I asked him for a copy. If you have youngsters of your own or grandchildren, I believe you will appreciate it as well.

First, a mother is speaking: "Dear Teacher: Please find attached to this note one six-year-old boy, much cleaner and quieter than usual and with a new hair cut and blue jeans. With him go the prayers of his mother and father. He's good at creating airplanes and chaos, very adept at tying knots and attracting stray dogs; he especially likes peanut butter, horses, the westerns, empty boxes and his shirt tail out. He is allergic to baths, bedtime, taking out the trash, and coming the first time he's called. He needs to be taught and spanked, loved and spanked, and reminded to blow his nose and come straight home from school. After having him in your class and on your nerves, you may not be the same, but I believe you will be glad to know him because while he strews books, toys and clothes, he has a special way of scattering happiness. Written, I'm afraid, with prejudice. Signed, his Mother."

Here's the principal's response: "Dear Mother: Please find attached to this diploma one eighteen-year-old boy, much more mature, with loftier ideals and goals than he had when you sent him to us some twelve years ago. With him go the prayers of his teachers and friends. He's good at different things now. He has more understanding of the world about him. He is able to do mathematical computations, knows something of the scientific approach to problem solving. He can read and write in at least the English language, and has probably developed some skills in typing, woodworking, art, and driving an automobile. He is still allergic to baths, bedtime, taking out the trash and coming the first time he's called. He still needs to be taught and loved, but perhaps not spanked. He needs to be reminded of the adult responsibilities of adult membership in the American society, to uphold the ideals of good citizenship, integrity, honesty, justice, humility, and priority of life. He needs to realize that the completely successful life involves a partnership with his family, his community and his God. He should be told that education is a never-ending process and only begins at the school house door. After having him in our classes and on our nerves, we are not the same! We're better people, enriched by his presence, broader in our understanding of humanity for having known him. We think we have provided him with an unbounded opportunity to learn in an atmosphere that has as its principle purpose the development of well-informed citizens who carry on the great traditions of America. We love him, too. Written also with prejudice. Signed, his principal."

To amplify my own sentiments with respect to this excellent article, every freedom-loving American needs to take a positive attitude towards the schools in this nation, and do what we can to make them better in the years to come.

When love and skill work together, expect a masterpiece.

John Ruskin

The nation that has the schools has the future.

Bismark

Courtesy Never Costs
—It Pays

*Are you a courteous person? Those truly
courteous in their dealings with others,
will find many doors opening for them, and
it's also a sign of good breeding. However,
genuine courtesy goes far beyond the
obvious. It's much more than permitting
others to break in line at the cafeteria,
the supermarket check-out stand, or even
saying, "Here, let me get that for you."*

The other evening the phone rang at our
house and a very pleasant-sounding young woman
was on the line attempting to enlist subscribers for a

new magazine. After she introduced herself and the product she was selling, she went into her sales pitch. I listened very attentively and when she finished, I told her I had read a previous issue of her magazine and liked it, but due to some commitments in other areas, I didn't want to subscribe at that time. She thanked me very politely and hung up the phone.

Now, you may say, "What's so unusual about this conversation with a telephone solicitor?" Well, you be the judge, but in light of what I've been hearing the past few years, apparently a lot of people are very rude to solicitors when they call. In many cases, they yell at them, swear at them, or just slam the receiver down in their ear. I'm convinced some people are rude by nature and extend this form of discourtesy to everyone they are around. Others feel they are being harassed and they develop a "mind set" to telephone solicitors and just turn them off. On the other hand, many people have been unduly influenced by negative comments made by their family or friends about telephone solicitors.

If you are in the habit of doing this, I want to share some thoughts with you that may cause you to change your thinking. The reasons will become obvious as you read on. In the end, I hope you will see that courtesy never costs—it pays, and here are some reasons why this is true.

A lot of people who are rude never stop to realize the American free enterprise system is based on sales, and this includes sales made over the telephone. Without sales our whole economic system slows down, and in time this puts many people out of work. But you say, "If I want to buy something, I will call them or go to a store." While this is true, just stop for a moment and think about where the money you have in the bank came from. It also came from sales and some of those sales were made over the telephone.

When the young woman I mentioned makes a sale, think about the chain reaction that takes place. She gets a paycheck, as do others in her company. They can take their earnings and pay house payments, car payments, and utility bills. They can buy groceries, eat out once in a while, and go to a movie. God only knows what all that money will be spent for. As I say, sales keep our economic system moving and, either directly or indirectly, we all benefit.

I hope the next time someone calls trying to sell you something, if you are not by nature a courteous person, you will remember what I've said and be thoughtful and considerate of the salesperson's feelings. You don't have to yell, swear, or hang up; just very calmly and politely say, "I'm sorry, I'm not interested in what you are selling, but I appreciate your calling." Should the salesperson persist or call back, again very calmly say, "I've made a decision, but if you want to invest your time and money in this way, that's up to you." You will be amazed at what this will do for you and the caller. My friend, it's true: it doesn't cost a penny to be courteous and it will pay you a tremendous dividend for your time and energy.

> *If a man be gracious and courteous to strangers, it shows he is a citizen of the world.*
>
> Francis Bacon

Attitude

Our Attitudes Control Our Lives

William James of Harvard University, the father of American psychology, once said, "The greatest discovery of my generation is that human beings can alter their lives by altering their attitudes of mind." This profound statement made many years ago contains tremendous potential to help us become happier and more successful human beings. After all, isn't this what most of us want our lives to be?

My wife has a sweatshirt with the words "I have an attitude" printed across the front. To symbolize the word "attitude" there is also a picture of a duck with the most awful facial configuration you can imagine. The dictionary defines "attitude" as "a state of mind or feeling." Unlike computers, which can only store facts, statistics and other data, the human mind also has the capability of storing feelings and emotions.

The marvelous human mind with its many and diverse powers is what produces thoughts, and these thoughts become the basis for our actions. Our actions, therefore, are the result of not only what we think, but also how we feel. It's important to realize (as it relates to your personal success), that actions trigger feelings and feelings trigger actions.

Your thoughts and feelings produce "attitudes." As Dr. James points out, "human beings can alter their lives by altering their attitudes of mind."

There have been a number of people and organizations who have conducted studies to determine the basis for personal success and they all pretty much conclude the same thing. Mental attitude accounts for about eight-five percent of our overall success in life, while skills and knowledge make up the balance.

I would like to share a true-life experience that can help you see how important mental attitude really is and why it controls our lives. In the 1958 World Series between the New York Yankees and the Milwaukee Brewers, during the late innings of a very crucial game, Elston Howard, power-hitting Yankee catcher, was up to bat. With the count three balls and two strikes, the Braves' manager went out to the mound to talk with Warren Spahn, his great left-handed pitcher. The manager said, "Don't give him a high outside pitch, because he will hit it out of the park!" and returned to the dugout.

It was too late! Warren's computer-like mind registered the thought "high outside pitch," which is exactly where the ball went. The manager was right; Elston Howard hit it out of the park! As Elston circled the bases, Warren Spahn threw his glove down in the dirt and made what has become a classic statement. He said, "Why would anyone motivate themselves or others with the reverse of an idea?"

You see, because of the way the human mind is constituted, we always move in the direction of our currently dominant thought. The chances that Warren Spahn would have been successful in pitching to Elston Howard would have been greatly increased if the manager had simply said, "Keep the ball low and inside."

The reason attitudes control our lives is simple. We always move in the direction of our currently dominant thought. When we are thinking good and true things and have worthy goals to strive for, our attitude becomes one of our best friends.

> *It's your attitude, and not your aptitude,*
> *that will determine your altitude.*
>
> Bob Gannaway

> *Be true to the best you know, if you*
> *do your best you cannot do more. Do*
> *your best every day and your life will*
> *gradually expand into satisfying fullness.*
>
> Author unknown

Chance

The Lincoln—Kennedy Amazing Coincidences

After I read the following article that I'm about to share with you, I was reminded of the words of Satchel Paige: "Don't look back, something may be gaining on you."

Over the years in writing and producing my daily radio program, I've produced a number of shows on the life of Abraham Lincoln, a man whom I consider to be one of America's greatest presidents. After one of these shows had aired on a local station, I received a phone call from a listener who said, "Have you ever heard of the amazing coincidences between Abraham Lincoln and John

F. Kennedy?" When I confessed I had not, she offered to send a copy of the article to me.

When I read the amazing coincidences between these two slain American Presidents, I was astounded, because it was not only amazing, it also gave me a very eerie feeling. In the event you have never read or heard this story, I would like to pass it along to you. I believe you will find it quite interesting.

Lincoln was elected in 1860, Kennedy was elected in 1960, exactly one hundred years apart.

There are seven letters in each name.

Both presidents were slain on Friday; both men were slain in the presence of their wives.

Both were directly concerned with civil rights.

Both presidents had legality of elections contested.

Kennedy's secretary's name was Lincoln, who warned him not to go to Dallas; Lincoln's secretary's name was Kennedy, who warned him not to go to the theater.

Both of their successors' names were Johnson: Andrew Johnson and Lyndon Johnson. Each name contains thirteen letters; both men served in the U.S. Senate; both were southern Democrats.

Andrew Johnson was born in 1808, and Lyndon Johnson was born in 1908.

Booth and Oswald were both southerners favoring unpopular ideas. Oswald shot Kennedy from a warehouse and hid in a theater; Booth shot Lincoln in a theater and hid in a warehouse. Booth and Oswald were both murdered before a trial could be arranged. Booth and Oswald were born one hundred years apart, and each name— Lee Harvey Oswald and John Wilkes Booth, has fifteen letters.

Well, what do you think? I'll confess I don't know what to make of it. It is highly unusual. While we live in a world of order, what do you think the chances or the odds would be that this would ever occur again?

Coincidence is Chance stumbling more
than once in the same place.

D.W. Allen

Early Settlers

Mountain Talk

William Smith, the father of English geology, once said, "Language is the memory of the human race." In recent times, progress and advancement in education have altered the course of human history. When it could be truthfully said "the pen was mightier than the sword," the fulcrum of power was no longer brute strength, but people's ability to use their native tongue with grace and ease. While America is a land of diverse peoples and cultures, our rich heritage is something we should always strive to preserve.

Several years ago, I had the privilege of being the speaker for the Yellville, Arkansas, Chamber of Commerce Banquet. Yellville is a quiet little town on the Ozark Mountain plateau. The morning following my speech, I had breakfast at a little restaurant called the Cedar Inn. I understand it's no longer in business but their placemats contained something called "Mountain Talk" I found to be very interesting.

Before I share this with you, let me point out or at least emphasize that one of the greatest things about our country is that we have a common bond. Regardless of who our ancestors were or where they came from; what we do for a living; whether we are rich or poor; we are all Americans. We are all citizens of the greatest nation in the world.

Not only do we all have a common bond, we also have a great diversity among our people which is also a great strength. As diversity relates to our language, millions of American speak languages in addition to English and many speak with an accent. Accents can reflect more than Americans' ethnic variety—they can reveal regional speech patterns as well.

"Mountain Talk," the article from the placemat I want to share with you, contains regional sayings commonly used in the Ozark Mountain area.

Some of these sayings have roots in expressions found in England, Scotland and Ireland brought to this country by early settlers who lived in mountain regions of the American South. Here are some of the examples:

A-fixin' means getting ready to do something. "We're a-fixin' to go to the store."

Peaked means pale or sickly looking. "He's looking mighty peaked today."

Fetch means to bring. "Go fetch the doctor."

Put out means angry or annoyed. "He shore was put out about the meeting."

Hesh-up means become quiet. "Make Jamie hesh-up."

Clum means climbed. "I clum that hill for the last time."

Now before I'm plum slap done, I would like to give you more of the sayings without the definitions and examples. You will probably be able to figure out some of them.

Askeered of; doins; dast; holler; vittles; you'uns; cuttin' up; book read; fur piece; gully washer; lolly gag; pizen; crick; airish; kiver; skittish; and smack dab.

These expressions have a way of touching my roots, and, if you will think about it, you can probably trace yours back there, too. You know if we take this line of thinking back far enough, we're all just chips off the old block.

> *All speech, written or spoken, is a dead language until it finds a willing and prepared hearer.*
>
> Robert Louis Stevenson

Love

One Set of Footprints

Someone has said, "The person who does not stand for something will fall for anything," and I certainly believe this is true. If there is one thing in this life that I have placed my complete trust and faith in, it's that there is an all-wise, all-powerful and ever-present God, and that He loves and cares for me!

I was reminded of this dynamic truth one day recently, while visiting in a friend's office. In the course of my work, I travel a great deal and I stopped by to see a friend who lives in the beautiful Ozark Mountain community of Harrison, Arkansas. We were just sitting there chatting and I noticed something hanging on his wall titled, "One Set of Footprints."

The story has been around for a long time but it was new to me.

You may already be familiar with this story, but it contains such a touching and profound message, I would like to share it with you.

One Set of Footprints

One night a man had a dream. He dreamed he was walking along the beach with the Lord. Across the sky flashed scenes from his life. For each scene he noticed two sets of footprints in the sand, one belonging to him and the other belonging to the Lord.

When the last scene had flashed before him, he looked back at the footprints and noticed that many times along the path, there was only one set of footprints in the sand. He also noticed this happened during the lowest and saddest times of his life.

This really bothered him, so he questioned the Lord. "Lord, you said once I decided to follow you, you would walk all the way, but I noticed that during the most troublesome times of my life, there was only one set of footprints. I don't understand why. When I needed you most, you deserted me."

The Lord replied, "My precious child, I love you, and would never leave you. During your times of trial and suffering, when you see only one set of footprints, it was then that I carried you."

After reading this story, I asked my friend to make a copy of it, and I've shared it with our radio audience, and many other people since then. As I look around me, I am amazed at the handiwork and power of God; to have the complete assurance of His Word; and that He is still in control.

Next time you are faced with trials and tribulations, especially during those low times in your life, I hope you will remember the story, "One Set of Footprints." One of my greatest joys in knowing God in a personal way, is to know that He is faithful, and will be there to carry me during those times when I need Him most. If you do not have this peace in your heart, believe me, my friend, there is no greater joy in all the world.

He who believes in God is not careful
for the morrow, but labors joyfully and
with a great heart. 'For he giveth his
beloved as in sleep.' They must work and
watch, yet never be careful or anxious,
but commit all to him, and live in serene
tranquility; with a quiet heart, as one
who sleeps safely and quietly.

Martin Luther

Leadership

Your Decisions Will Affect Your Family

Since the beginning of recorded history, the family has always been one of the essential building blocks in the success of an empire or a nation. The late William Thayer expressed it this way: "If well ordered, they are the springs from which go forth the streams of national greatness and prosperity, of civil order and public happiness." As leaders in the home of America, our decisions will often affect our family for years to come.

According to the Bible I've been reading for the past several years, not one of us is perfect.

For example, in Romans 3:23 it says, "For all have sinned and come short of the glory of God," and I know this is true. While I'm not perfect and I'm certainly not a preacher, it's my heart's desire to share something with you that will help you become a happier, richer and more successful person. To do this, sometimes all we need is to be reminded of those things most important to us.

Some time ago, I heard a true story I believe can have a tremendous bearing on the traditional family in the years to come. In the seventeenth century there were two families in America by the names of Edwards and Jukes. As the head of the Edwards family, Mr. Edwards was a godly man and he did his best to provide spiritual leadership and also to be a productive and law-abiding member of society. Mr. Jukes, on the other hand, was more or less a common criminal, spending much of his time in jail, and was anything but a good example for others to follow.

Several years ago, someone did a study on the history of these two families, and here is what they found. The Edwards family produced the famous minister, Jonathan Edwards, who entered Yale University at the age of thirteen and later became a great theologian and author of several books. Further research revealed the Edwards' family tree contained a long list of ministers, college presidents and other prominent members of society.

Research on the Jukes family revealed the virtues of the original Mr. Jukes were passed on to his offspring. The Jukes' family consisted of many criminals and others of unsavory character.

If you are the leader in your home, the kind of person you are and the decisions you make will affect your family. If you are living the kind of life of which you are not proud, and have personal vices and habits that would keep you from being a good role model, it does not necessarily mean that your children will turn out the same way. People with this kind of background have risen above their circumstances to become outstanding successes. In no way do I want you to take what I'm saying too personally, because we all have problems, burdens and challenges, but there is a principle we should all consider: "What's true in the root will be seen in the fruit." There is a lot of truth in the saying, "Like father, like son."

The one thing our children want from us more than anything else is our approval, and they will often go to great lengths to get it. This is a free country where we have the opportunities to make our own choices and decisions that affect our lives. Keep in mind, however, your decisions will affect your family, and they will often have consequences for many years to come.

Making decisions is simple: get the facts, seek God's guidance, form a judgment, act on it, worry no more.

Charles E. Bennett

The fear of the Lord is the beginning of knowledge, but fools despise wisdom and instruction.

Proverbs 1:7 (NKJV)

Success

"And Then Some..."

We hear a great deal these days about the "secrets of success." In reality, this is simply a marketing gimmick used to sell many of the success programs produced today. True success can be summed up by these words of former President Harry S. Truman: "I studied the lives of great men and famous women, and I found that the men and women who got to the top were those who did the jobs they had in hand, with everything they had of energy, enthusiasm and hard work." As a starting point, you show me someone who is lazy, and I'll show you a failure.

Some time ago, I had a wonderful, unique experience that brought this truth home to me in a very real way. During a *How to Plan Your Life* seminar at one of the many high schools where I've been privileged to work, I met a young man named Danny Sanders. Danny was a member of the senior class and a few weeks later, to my surprise, I received a three-page, hand-written letter from him. Just the fact that a high school senior had taken the time to write was very gratifying, but he shared something in his letter that may be of value to you.

In his letter, Danny told about a young man who had become very successful at a young age. When someone asked him how he did it, he said, "And then some." When this person asked him what he meant, he replied, "When I was in school, when my teachers asked me to do something, I did it, and then some. Later, when I got a job, when my employer told me to do something (notice where I went from asking to telling), I did it, *and then some.* Finally, when I started a business of my own, I did what my customers expected, and then some."

This successful young man had been applying the universal law of cause and effect. This law, simply stated, means that for every cause there must be an effect, and for every effect there must be a cause. By rendering more service than was actually required, he was using this universal law to get more rewards in return.

When it comes to achieving success, one of the biggest mistakes many people make is wanting the rewards before they render the service. This could be compared to a man standing in front of a cold stove and saying, "Give me some heat, and then I will put in the wood."

Yes, a real understanding and application of this universal law which has been stated "And then some," will give you everything on earth you desire. If you are having trouble making ends meet, or having trouble in school or on your job, pause here and ask yourself this question: "Am I doing everything that is expected of me with the right attitude, and then some?"

When you apply this principle of the success of a business, that little extra and then some is the profit, and without earning a profit, you know what the outcome will be. Thanks to Danny, you and I have been reminded of that and I hope it's been of value to you, too.

Men and times change, but principles—never!
Grover Cleveland

The first and last thing required of genius is the love of truth.
Goethe

Discouragement: One of Our Greatest Enemies

People cannot do their best when they are deeply discouraged. Each of us should spend some time and learn what causes discouragement and what steps we can take to avoid or overcome it—that is, if we want to achieve outstanding success.

To achieve anything in life really worthwhile, there comes a time we refer to as "the moment of truth." Along the way, as we begin to struggle and maybe even have serious doubts, it's that critical time when we either give up or keep going. If you will examine this statement, I believe you will conclude the reason many people give up far short of achieving success, is because they become discouraged. On the other hand, those who keep going are those who find a source of inner strength which enables them to defeat or overcome discouragement.

It's natural and even necessary to give up on some things, especially if our priorities are wrong or the odds are too great. To be sure, I've given up many times. I remember a very vivid example when I was selling printing for a living. I had called on one particular man for months, and he never bought anything from me. Finally, I realized that he was never going to buy from me, so I gave up on him.

I could give you many other examples where this is true, but I believe you see my point. The key to success in most anything is to know when to give up and when to keep going. More often than not, however, the thing that keeps most people from achieving success is they give up too quickly.

There is a vast difference in giving up on reaching a specific goal (which is really the definition of success), and giving up on life in general. There is usually no real tragedy when we give up on a specific goal, but there is a real tragedy when we give up on life. If you are a person who has a tendency to become deeply discouraged, I want to help you, and I believe I can, by reminding you of the source of discouragement. Please think about this story I heard some time ago.

Once upon a time, Satan, growing old and weary decided it was time for him to retire from active work. He offered all of his devilish inventory of tools for sale to the highest bidders. At the time of the auction, the tools were all neatly arranged: envy, malice, enmity, sensuality, deceit and all of the other devices of evil. Each was plainly marked, and the price was surprisingly low, except for the ungainly piece of much-used steel marked 'discouragement.' It was priced ten times more than any of the other tools.

"Why, Mr. Satan," asked a prospective buyer, "do you ask so much for this tool?"

"Well," replied the old tempter, "this tool has always been my most useful one. You can see that it has more wear than any of the others. I can use it as a wedge to get into a person's mind and defeat him, when all other means fail."

If this story has any truth in it, we can plainly see Satan is the source of discouragement. He wants us to give up, sit down and wallow around in self-pity. If we allow this to happen, we certainly won't accomplish worthwhile things for God, our fellow man, or anyone else, including ourselves.

The only way to overcome discouragement is by intelligent action. Once you decide to do something worthwhile and get started, you'll soon find discouragement will leave you. God has given us a will, and in America we have the freedom and the opportunity to make choices. In every important decision in life, God votes for us, Satan votes against us, and it's left up to us to break the tie!

This is the beginning of a new day. God has given me this day to use as I will. This day is important because I am exchanging a day of my life for it. When tomorrow comes this day will be gone forever, leaving in its place something that I have traded for it. Therefore, I want it to be good and not evil, gain and not loss, success and not failure, in order that I shall not regret the price that I have paid for it.

Heartsill Wilson

A Few Dollars
and a Dream

*When our forefathers were establishing this
nation, they never intended we should all
be equal. Rather, their goal was for every
individual to have equal opportunity. This
simple philosophy or concept has produced
more "rags to riches" success stories, than
any other economic system in the history
of the world. If we don't see opportunity all
around us, in most cases it's not because it's
not there; it's because we can't see it.*

Do you have any idea what it takes to get
ahead financially in this country? I can answer in

just six words: *a few dollars and a dream.* There is a story behind these six words that has given them a very special meaning and I believe it will also give you something worthwhile to think about. When the United States of America was celebrating the one hundredth birthday of the Statue of Liberty, many true-life stories came to light about people who had come to this country with little more than the shirts on their backs, but over the years had become highly successful.

The story I mentioned is about Casey Rowe. Casey Rowe came to America from South Korea, some time after the Great Depression. At the time, all he had was a wife, seven children and $700. As he said, all he had was "a few dollars and a dream." He had no job, no friends, and, except for a few personal items, he had nothing else.

His first job was as an ax grinder. At night he would come home so tired he would literally cry himself to sleep, only to get up and do it all over again the next day. But Casey Rowe did not give up and he worked and worked and saved a small portion of what he earned.

His close family relationships gave him great emotional strength and courage and before many years had passed, he had saved enough money to go into business for himself. Today, if you go to the Terminal Building in Philadelphia, Pennsylvania, you will find Casey Rowe and his family hard at work in the produce business at four a.m., and the whole family works. They do over a million dollars' worth of business each year!

I'm sure many people who do business at their produce market have no idea of the tremendous struggle and the years of hard work it took for their business to prosper as it's doing today.

It's easy for casual observers to say, "Oh, these people are hard workers," or "They had money to begin with," or "They inherited the business." For people who have never achieved financial success, they either don't want it, or haven't been willing to pay the price for it. The saddest part of all, are the millions of people who have opportunity all around them, but have never been able to see it or develop sufficient belief in themselves to go after it.

The fact that Casey Rowe came from another country may have been as asset, because life where he came from may have been harder than it is here. On the other hand, we know of thousands of people who come from other countries who do not achieve financial success. Many of these people have returned home broke and discouraged, while others stay but have to struggle to survive.

The message of Casey Rowe's story is simple. If you want to achieve greater financial success, all you need is *a few dollars and a dream,* and then be willing to work hard for the next ten to twenty years to make your dream come true. While it may be harder today to save a portion of what you earn, because of inflation and higher taxes, saving a portion of your income is the key. Without demonstrating the self-discipline to set aside a portion of your earnings in the beginning, the people who have resources to help you are not likely to take a chance. In most cases, the only way you can borrow enough money to get started, is to prove that you don't really need it.

> *Go confidently in the direction of your dreams! Live the life you've imagined! As you simplify your life, the laws of the universe will be simpler, solitude will not be solitude, poverty will not be poverty, nor weakness weakness.*
>
> Henry David Thoreau

Hit a Stroke
and Drag Charlie

*In Australia, the Aborigines perform an
ancient custom of beating the ground with
clubs and uttering wild and terrifying
sounds. According to anthropologists, this is
a manifestation of primitive self-expression.
When the same practice takes place in the
United States, we have another name for
it—golf!*

The other day, a friend told me a story I
believe anyone who loves the game of golf will
enjoy. It seems two middle-aged men, Bill and
Charlie, decided to take up the game of golf as a

way to stay in shape. After the decision was made, the first thing they had to do was go to the sporting goods store to buy some equipment. After a lengthy discussion with the store manager, they finally settled on a new set of clubs, shoes, pants, shirts and socks to match, a new hat, tees and the best golf balls in the store.

That same afternoon, Bill and Charlie met at the local course for their first round of golf, each man decked out in his new outfit and sporting brand new clubs. No doubt about it, they were sharp! In fact, they were the envy of everyone around the clubhouse. From the beginning, however, it was obvious they were going to need some help with their game. After a dozen or so swings from the practice tee, Bill looked at Charlie and Charlie looked at Bill, until finally Bill suggested, "Why don't we hire the 'pro' to give us a few lessons?"

With a few lessons, it didn't take long at all until Bill and Charlie were hitting straight down the middle of the fairway. The pro also stayed around long enough to help them work on their short game. They learned how to select the proper irons, how to loft the ball to the green to make it bite, how to pitch and run, and most importantly, they learned how to putt. As the pro explained, this was the 'money' game, because no person would ever become a great golfer if he couldn't master the art of putting.

Off to a good start, Bill and Charlie began to play on a regular basis. They set aside every Thursday afternoon to play golf. Over the next several months, they both found they loved the game and were getting much better at it. As a bonus, they were also feeling much better which was the original purpose for taking up the game. With scores that started out well over 100, it wasn't long until they were both shooting in the mid to high 80s on a consistent basis.

At this point, they decided to also play on Saturday mornings, in addition to Thursday afternoons. Still they continued to improve, occasionally shooting rounds in the high 70s. Now they were really getting serious. Thursday afternoons and Saturday mornings were increased to include Sunday afternoons, then Monday afternoons as the torrid pace continued. Still their rounds continued to improve.

Now they were breaking par on a regular basis. Because they were well-known, they soon became the talk of the town. A lot of their friends and even strangers, would stop them on the street and ask, "What did you shoot today?" One day Bill said, "I shot a 69—my best ever." Then Charlie said, "Would you believe it? I shot a 67," which was even two strokes better than Bill.

A few months later on a hot July day, Bill was walking down the street alone, and a friend came up and said, "What did you shoot today Bill?"

Bill said, "I shot an 86."

The friend who knew of Bill's golfing reputation was amazed and he said, "Why did you shoot so high?"

Bill said, "Well, this morning on the fifth hole, Charlie passed out on me, and for the rest of the round, it was hit a stroke and drag Charlie!"

Passion is a sort of fever in the mind,
which leaves us weaker than it found us.
William Penn

The master passion is hunger for
self-approval.

Mark Twain

That One Little Thing Called a T-o-n-g-u-e

My good friend, Doyle Burke, from Newport, Arkansas, always has several funny stories to share with me each time I see him, but some time ago I saw him when he was almost speechless. It was at the Convention Center in Little Rock on the day he received a plaque to mark his retirement from the education profession. He was asked to say a few words before six hundred of his peers. He simply stated, "It is better to remain silent and have people assume you are a fool, than to speak and no longer have them assume it."

The ability to speak is a wonderful gift that God has given us and for those who can develop it to a high degree of proficiency, it can bring all sorts of rewards. If I were to ask you to state in one word the most powerful part of the human body as it relates to speaking and communication, what would be your answer? If you said the little six letter word called a t-o-n-g-u-e, you'd be right.

The reason I believe this is true is because I have seen the tongue lift the spirits and motivate a 260-pound man to action, and I have seen another tongue slash a person to shreds. Yes, the tongue is a very powerful thing, and learning to control it is a goal worthy for any person. The tongue is like a two-edged sword—one side is good and the other side is bad. It's how we choose to use it that makes the difference. It's only when we learn to control our tongue and use it for good that we can rightfully expect good things to happen in our lives.

In my own experience, I have found many people have Dr. Jekyll/Mr. Hyde personalities in respect to their tongues. When they are in public or "on stage," so to speak, they use their tongues one way, but when they are "off stage," you would never know they were the same people.

The Bible says in Matthew 15:18, "But those things that proceed out of the mouth come forth from the heart and they defile the man." So, there you have it.

It is really the heart of a man or woman which determines what comes out of his or her mouth. The tongue, on the other hand, is just a protrusive, freely moving organ that in human beings serves as an organ of taste and speech. I believe if you will give this some serious thought, you will see it is not smart or intelligent people, or even those who are gifted with unusual skills, that learn to control and use their tongues wisely. It is the people whose hearts are right, who exercise self-control and learn to speak only those things which serve to build lasting relationships.

If you have a problem controlling your tongue and you want to do something about it, a good place to start is to examine your heart. When you get your heart right with others, it will be much easier to control your tongue. I always admire a soft-spoken, gentle person who speaks the truth and is always positive when talking about others. There just seems to be an inner strength that says it's not necessary to tear others down to build themselves up.

Wouldn't this world be a much better place if everyone would strive to be that kind of person? Of course, you know a better world must begin with you and me!

Jim Davidson

One reason why a dog is such a lovable creature is that his tail wags instead of his tongue.

Author unknown

The High Cost of Getting Even

When it comes to forgiving others for wrongs they have committed against us, Henry Ward Beecher said: "I can forgive, but I cannot forget." It is only another way of saying, "I cannot forgive." We see still others who say, "I don't get mad, I get even," but do we really and truly ever 'get even'?

We have all heard some people say, I'm going to get even with that so-and-so, if it's the last thing I ever do!" after they have been hurt or wronged in some way. You may have made this statement yourself. I know I've said this in the past before I learned what it was doing to me. Sometimes we make statements like this in a flash of anger but don't really mean them. In this case, the situation passes and we are able to recover emotionally without too much damage. However, there are some situations where the people involved really do mean it and their emotions begin to 'fester,' and over a period of time, it exacts a heavy toll.

Dr. S. I. McMillion has done a great deal of research about the attitude of "getting even," and has concluded that ulcers, high blood pressure, strokes and most other physical maladies are connected to harboring resentment, hatred and ill will toward others. He says it might be truthfully written on many thousands of death certificates that the victim died from "grudgeitis."

Dr. McMillion makes a good case to show how hatred enslaves the one who hates by employing the following allegory: "The moment I started hating a man, I became his slave. I cannot enjoy my work anymore because he even controls my thoughts. My resentments produce too many stress hormones in my body. I become fatigued after only a few hours of work. The man I hate hounds me wherever I go. I can't escape his tyrannical grasp of my mind. Whenever the waiter serves me porterhouse steak with French fries, asparagus, crisp salad and strawberry shortcake smothered with ice cream, it might as well be stale bread and water. My teeth chew the food, I swallow it, but the man I hate keeps me from enjoying it. The man I hate may be miles from my bedroom, but, more cruel than any slave driver, he whips my thoughts into such a frenzy that my inner spring mattress becomes a rack of torture. I really must acknowledge the fact that I am a slave to every man on whom I pour my wrath."

Hatred, like many of our other emotions, comes in degrees. The range can be all the way from a mild dislike to a deep burning desire to see the other person completely done in. Of course, in many cases, hatred results in violence, which means running afoul of the law. When this happens, and a person is convicted of a criminal offense, it means he has lost the opportunity to have complete control over his life.

In the interest of helping you be happier and more successful, be honest with yourself, and determine in your heart whether you really hate another person. If you do, then you know what the long-range consequences can be. There is only one solution to this universal problem and it's to be found in these words spoken by the man, Jesus. He said, "You have heard that it was said that you shall love your neighbor and hate your enemy, but I say unto you, love your enemy and pray for them that despitefully use you."

Whether we like it or not, the only thing that will free us of hatred is complete and total forgiveness. The biggest problem in this area that most of us face can be found in the answer to this question: "Who is my neighbor?"

Hating people is like burning down the barn to get rid of the rats. It's a case of the solution being much worse than the problem.

Author unknown

How to Tell a Winner from a Loser

The legendary football coach Vince Lombardi once said, "Winning is not the main thing, it is the only thing." Over the years, many people have misinterpreted Coach Lombardi's statement to mean winning at all costs, even if it meant not playing by the rules. Nothing could be further from the truth. The coach was talking about the will to win and the desire to win, but within the context of decency and fair play.

Let me share an article with you titled "How to Tell a Winner from a Loser," written by

Dr. Witt Schultz. While not written from an athletic perspective, this article is about the much larger "game of life," and should be useful in helping us determine where we are.

How to Tell a Winner from a Loser

A winner says, "Let's find out." A loser says, "Nobody knows."

When a winner makes a mistake, he says, "I was wrong." When a loser makes a mistake, he says, "It wasn't my fault."

A winner credits his good luck for winning, even though it isn't good luck. A loser blames his bad luck for losing, even though it isn't bad luck.

A winner knows how to say "yes" and "no." A loser says, "yes, but" and "perhaps not," at the wrong times for the wrong reasons.

A winner works harder than a loser and has more. A loser is always too busy to do what is necessary.

A winner works through a problem. A loser goes around it and never gets past it.

A winner makes commitments, a loser makes promises.

A winner shows he is sorry by making up for it. A loser says, "I'm sorry," but he does the same thing next time around.

A winner knows what to fight for and when to compromise. A loser compromises when he shouldn't and fights for what isn't worthwhile.

A winner says, "I'm good, but not as good as I ought to be." A loser says, "I'm not as bad as a lot of other people."

A winner listens, a loser just waits until it's his turn to talk.

A winner feels strong enough to be gentle. A loser is never gentle; he is either weak or pettily tyrannous by turns.

A winner explains, a loser explains away.

A winner feels responsible for more than his job. A loser says, "I only work here."

A winner says, "There ought to be a better way to do it." A loser says, "That's the way it's always been done."

A winner paces himself, a loser has only two speeds: hysterical and lethargic.

For me, this article by Dr. Witt Schultz really hits home. Does it also speak to you? Because we are creatures of habit, we sometimes permit ourselves to fall into a mental rut, and we just act on those thoughts that have become ingrained in our subconscious minds.

Of course, people we spend our time with have a great impact on our lives because they are the ones who are feeding our minds. Over the years, I have learned never to pin a label on someone, especially a label like 'loser,' because it's such a powerful thing in determining a person's self-image. While it may not be realistic, it's my hope that every person could become a winner because our society would be a much better place for all of us. If you are not already a winner, why not begin at once to develop those winning habits and attitudes?

> *Great minds have noble objectives, high purposes, and daring dreams; average minds engage themselves in wishful thinking and petty dabblings in little ventures; small minds are content to complain why life has passed them by.*
>
> Author unknown

Responsibility

The One in the Glass

*Have you known people who had trouble
looking you straight in the eye? The reasons
are many. For some it may be shyness or
a lack of self-confidence; for others a guilt
complex or even a downcast feeling, because
of a poor self-image. It's tragic for any person
to go through life in this way, especially if this
person happens to be you or me.*

You know, many people go through life
running away from various circumstances or other
people. But there is one thing in this life that you
can't run away from, and that's *yourself.* I know full
well this is true in my own life. Regardless of where
I go, or what I do, I still have to deal with me.

Several years ago, I was talking with a gentleman and he made this comment: "It's been said that we should do unto others as we would have them do unto us," which has come to be known as the Golden Rule. To elaborate just a bit on the Golden Rule, it also means that we should love our neighbor as ourselves. This gentleman went on to say, "The reason many of us don't love our neighbor, is that we don't love ourselves."

Unfortunately, in many cases, this is true. There are millions of people in this country, and throughout the world, who look into the mirror everyday and just don't like what they see. Studies have revealed much of this dislike is not because the person is ugly or unattractive, but the result of a much deeper inner conflict. Along these lines, I would like to share a meaningful poem I ran across many years ago:

The One in the Glass

As you go through life in your struggle for
    self
And the world makes you king or queen for
    a day,
Just go to a mirror and look at yourself,
And see what that person has to say.
For it isn't your father or mother or spouse

Whose judgment upon you must pass;
But the one whose verdict counts most in
   your
Life is the one staring back from the glass.
Some people may think you're a straight
   shootin' sort
And call you a wonderful gal or guy,
But the one in the glass says you're only a
   bum
If you can't look him straight in the eye.
He or she is the one to please, never mind
   all the rest,
For they are with you clear up to the end,
And you have passed your most dangerous
   difficult task,
If the one in the glass is your friend.
You may fool the whole world down the
   pathway of Life
And get pats on the back as you pass,
But your final rewards will be heartaches
   and tears,
If you've cheated the one in the glass.

                              Author unknown

   The message that always comes through to
me as I read or hear "The One in the Glass," is
that sooner or later, I must use what God has given
me and accept full responsibility for my own life.

When we reach legal age and maturity, if we are fortunate enough to have a sound mind and body, no one should ever have to be responsible for us again.

> *It is impossible to cheat life. There are*
> *no answers to the problems of life in the*
> *back of the book.*
> > Soren Kierkegaard

> *Life is real! Life is earnest! And the*
> *grave is not its goal.*
> > Henry Wadsworth Longfellow

Motherhood

The Hand That Rocks the Cradle Rules the World

Show me a great leader, a gifted teacher, a successful business person, a devoted parent or anyone else who has made a real mark on the world, and in the vast majority of cases, I will show you people who learned their values from their mothers.

There is a saying, "The hand that rocks the cradle rules the world." This is true, but in light of our changing society, many of our nation's problems are the result of the hand rocking the cradle not being that of the child's mother. The economic pressures brought on by inflation and the emergence of the career woman has resulted in more and more mothers working outside the home. Consequently, the values of their children are being taught by others.

Now, this is not always bad, but any rational, thinking person would accept as a basic premise that young children's direction in life is more influenced by their mother's love, guidance and teaching before they reach the age of accountability than any other single factor.

However, we see exceptions to the rule almost everyday in our society. There are many cases when we know a child has the best parents to be found anywhere, yet the child still goes wrong. What you see is not always what you get. Many times, on the surface it appears a certain family epitomizes what the majority of our citizens think an "all American" family should be. The parents are leaders in their community, they are strong and faithful members of a church, they do things together as a family, but still there are key ingredients missing that keep their offspring from turning out to be productive, law-abiding members of society.

To be sure, in today's times, it is not easy to be a parent. There are pressures on our youngsters in the community, in school, and later on the job, that tear at the very fabric most God-fearing parents are trying to weave. Regardless of where a child gets his or her values, here is something to consider.

Children Learn What They Live

If a child lives with criticism, he learns to condemn.

If a child lives with hostility, he learns to fight.

If a child lives with ridicule, he learns to be shy.

If a child lives with shame, he learns to feel guilty.

If a child lives with tolerance, he learns to be patient.

If a child lives with encouragement, he learns confidence.

If a child lives with praise, he learns to appreciate.

If a child lives with fairness, he learns justice.

If a child lives with security, he learns to have faith.

If a child lives with approval, he learns to like himself.

If a child lives with acceptance and friendship, he learns to find love in the world.

This was written by Dorothy Law Nolte, and you have probably seen it before, but it's still a good reminder for those of us who love our children and want the very best for their lives. If you are in the process of rearing one or more of God's special gifts, give yourself a checkup, because the "hand that rocks the cradle," really does rule the world.

> *In acquiring knowledge there is one thing equally important, and that is character. Nothing in the world is worth so much, will last so long, and serve its possessor so well as good character.*
>
> William McKinley

> *Mother is the name for 'God' in the lips and hearts of little children.*
>
> William M. Thackeray

Communication

But the Bumble Bee
Can't Fly

The patrolman stopped a woman who was speeding. He asked to see her driver's license and said, "Lady, you were going fifty miles an hour in a thirty-five mile-an-hour zone." As she handed him her license, she said, "Before you begin writing that ticket, I think we should get our priorities straight. Are you supposed to advise me of my constitutional rights first, or am I supposed to tell you that my son is the head of the state highway patrol?"

As you read this humorous story, did you understand exactly what this lady had in mind?

If you did, then you have some insights into the process of communication. While she did not say so, it's obvious that she was trying to use her son's influence to avoid paying a speeding ticket. The ability to communicate is a wonderful gift and those in our society who develop it well have a tremendous advantage over those who don't.

As you think about the importance of communication in your own life, I would like to tell you another story involving communication that could have a tremendous bearing on your future. It's the story of the bumble bee. According to the theory of aerodynamics, the bumble bee is not supposed to be able to fly, because the size, weight and shape of his body, in relation to his wing span, makes flying impossible. But you see, here is the problem. Somebody forgot to tell the bumble bee and he goes ahead and flies and drills holes every day.

This story or example has been around for a long time, and while most people have heard it, I'm not sure they see the correlation between the bumble bee and themselves. The reason this is true is because we have the ability to communicate, while the bumble bee does not, and if someone who is an authority on the subject tells us that it's impossible to do something, we just accept it at face value.

Instead of going ahead and trying something new or difficult and giving it our best shot, we just pass it off by saying, "Well, you just can't do that." Let me make a quick distinction here. While some people attempt life-threatening or potentially dangerous feats, like jumping out of an airplane without a parachute or anything else that might be considered dare-devil, I'm talking about activities that could make us happier and more successful human beings.

About twenty years ago, when I first went into the sales profession, it didn't take me long to realize I had to steer clear of the older salesmen who had been around for years. Most of them were just plodding along and marking time. They were quick to tell me why a particular person or company would not buy from us.

Of course, many new salesmen listen to this kind of talk and they never go out and make the effort, or if they do, they take the first rejection as proof the older, more experienced salesmen were right. All through life, you will meet people who have tried things and failed, and they will be quick to tell you why you can't do it, either. In some cases, they may be right, but here is the principle the story about the bumble bee should teach us: If what you want to do has potential and merit and will help you achieve what you want to achieve, how are you going to know whether you can succeed or not, if you don't try it for yourself? I hope from this day forth you will always remember the story of the bumble bee. The bumble bee is not supposed to be able to fly—but he did!

> *Science is a first-rate piece of furniture*
> *for a man's upper chamber, if he has*
> *common sense on the ground floor.*
> Oliver Wendell Holmes

> *There are but two powers in the world,*
> *the sword and the mind. In the long run*
> *the sword is always beaten by the mind.*
> Napoleon Bonaparte

The Silent Patients Speak

*Have you ever thought about the thousands
of people in this country who spend
countless hours confined to a bed in
a hospital or a nursing home who, for
one reason or another, cannot speak for
themselves or make their wishes known?*

If I had family or loved ones in this condition, I would want to know they were receiving the best possible medical care, but I would also want to know the people who were taking care of them were thoughtful, tenderhearted and kind, especially in light of a touching article I read a while back. This article is titled, "The Silent Patients Speak" and it was written by Anita Wildhaver, a registered nurse. If you have never had a reason to contemplate the plight of people in this condition, I believe the message this article contains will speak to your heart.

The Silent Patients Speak

Though we can't speak, see, or move of our own will, we are living beings. We are your stroke patients, the brain damaged, and all your other patients, who by illness or injury are locked inside the dark, silent shells of our bodies. We can't cry out in pain or discomfort, regardless of how severe they are. We can't express anger, despair, disgust, nor even happiness. But, hear us, you walking, talking, feeling, doing beings. Some of us are aware. We hear, think and know. We are not living vegetables, nor do we think we would be 'better off dead.' We still have enough self-respect to be embarrassed at hearing your conversation about your personal problems and your sex lives.

We are frightened by your conversations that relate the latest gossip about the questionable ability of the doctor who is responsible for our care. For his knowledge must be used to save us if we are to ever recover. We feel shame at having our bodies exposed for any and all to see. It does matter to us that we lie in feces or urine for hours, and our muscles ache with pain from the strain of remaining in one position without being moved. We can feel our mouths filled with mucus, drying and caking to form ulcerated areas. We can feel the stomach cramps from ice cold tube feedings with all the speed and lack of concern of pouring water down the drain.

We can feel the pain of our skin breaking down from poor and careless nursing care. We can also feel joy—the joy derived from the firm, gentle touch of a person giving us good nursing care. We can rest more carefully, when we are bathed, when our mouths and lips are cleansed, when our bodies are correctly positioned, when good skin care is given, when our beds are made neat and straight. We can appreciate the kindness of words spoken directly to us, and not about us. We can appreciate being told when procedures are about to be done, before they are begun.

Thanks, Anita, I hope my sharing your insights here will help some of these dear people receive better care. The vast majority of people in the nursing profession are kind, thoughtful and considerate, and highly qualified from a medical stand point. Unfortunately, a small percentage are not. Then too, because of human nature, we all have bad days from time to time when we get up on the wrong side of the bed. Another group of people in every profession have so many personal problems and are so wrapped up in themselves, that they just don't think at all. In most cases, these people don't realize what they are doing to make life miserable for another human being.

As Will Rogers once said, "It's just as important to be reminded as it is to be educated." Sometimes, all it takes to make tremendous changes for the better is a simple reminder of things we know but have forgotten. If you know someone, either a nurse or a patient who might benefit from this article, why not take a moment and share it? It could result in some of the greatest blessings you have ever received.

> *Jesus said, I have told you all this so that you may find your Peace in me. You will find trouble in the world, but never lose Heart, I have conquered the world.*
>
> John 16:33

> *Kindness is "a language which the dumb can speak, the deaf can Understand."*
>
> C.N. Bovee

Faith

God Is Still in Control

A person's faith is a very private matter, but as I have studied the Bible over the years, one of the most reassuring things I have come to believe is regardless of the events and circumstances we see about us, God is still in control.

I believe every one should hear the concept, "God is still in control," from time to time. God is eternal and to understand His greatness and His awesome power is something we should not fear, but take comfort in. I was reminded of this truth in a new and dynamic way the other day when I read an article titled, "Perspective." The article was written by Reverend David C. Fisher, pastor of a church in Bloomington, Minnesota.

The article contained a large photograph of Reverend Fisher jogging one morning with a beautiful mountain in the background. The caption at the bottom read, "As he ran that morning, he thought about all that was happening in this little town."

Come along with us on a short trip and share Reverend Fisher's exhilarating experience. I hope you, too, will gain a new perspective and be reminded that God is truly in control.

"It was early morning as I put on my new jogging outfit and headed west toward the edge of town. The rising sun warmed my back as I turned the corner and crossed the river. The cobwebs began to clear from my mind. Once again, I rejoiced from that special exultation that comes from exercise at dawn. I swung west again and faced the monster hill at the edge of town. I had never come this way before and I was anxious to try this new challenge.

"Halfway up the hill, I began to have serious doubts. My legs felt as if spikes were being driven into them. My lungs seemed to be burning as I kept my eyes focused on the pavement. Each step I took made the snow-capped Mount Adams loom larger until the whole horizon seemed to be filled with its 12,000-foot majesty. The pain of running drained from my body, as I was filled with the wonder of God's creation! I topped the hill and ran past the airport. I glanced to the south and there stood Mount Hood and Mount St. Helens in equal splendor.

"As I headed home, I saw the awakening city before me and my thoughts turned to its buildings and people. I was struck with the contrast of the physical creation of God, and the struggle of life on this planet. I thought about a house where a young woman lived alone, abandoned by her husband; an apartment where two unmarried young people were living together; another house where religious differences were ripping a family apart; a house where divorce threatened to destroy the children; another house where alcohol had already crushed one of God's special creations; and still another cottage in which a widow grieved alone. I looked up to see the church rising above the trees. Then I realized God's redemptive power is still at work. Yes, God is still in control."

> *The best way to reply to an atheist is to give him a good dinner... then ask him if he believes there is a cook.*
>
> *Louis Mizer*

Habits

Doing Without: A Hard Lesson to Learn

Former President Franklin D. Roosevelt once said, "Any government, like any family, can for a year spend a little more than it earns. But you and I know the continuance of that habit means the poorhouse." This is another way of saying people who are successful have formed success habits, while people who are failing have developed failure habits.

From my observation, I think one of the hardest lessons for many people to learn in today's times is how to do without. It's not easy to do

116

without, especially when we see so many people around us who seem to get everything they want. However, this uniquely American penchant, which is often referred to as 'keeping up with the Joneses,' has pushed many people so far into debt that bankruptcy and financial collapse is a real possibility. The real problem with trying to keep up with the Joneses is about the time we think we are there, they refinance!

I'm fairly conservative. I don't believe in people over-extending themselves, buying things they cannot afford and putting themselves and their family at risk for the future. On the other hand, if people have the means or the 'where-with-all,' as we say, to have all the things they want and do all things they want to do, I think it's wonderful, because it's the American dream. So long as their incomes are derived from legal means, I wish them continued success.

But we see thousands of people, perhaps millions, who want to live this kind of lifestyle, but they simply cannot afford it because they don't have any money. As a result, many of these people suffer from tension, stress, high blood pressure, and finally a stroke or heart attack or some other calamity.

I'm not talking about taking a calculated risk when it comes to getting ahead financially, because that's what financial success is all about. I'm simply talking about those people who have formed the habit of spending more than they earn, and there's a big difference. There are many reasons why we see people in our society who want to live 'high on the hog' without having the income to support it. It really comes down to the fact that they have never learned the habit of doing without. If you or someone you love happens to fit in this category, here are a few thoughts that may help:

> Fret not at small beginnings; the oak tree began as an acorn; the beautiful rainbow had its beginning in a drop of rain and a ray of light; the muscular athlete had trouble crawling; the university graduate started in first grade; the massive international oil industry began with a small shallow well.

In our country, it's still possible for most of us to have the things we want, but it may require a change in our thinking and our attitudes. Instead of 'buy now, pay later,' we must 'save and invest now, buy later.' Most people who really get ahead financially don't ever have to touch the principal of their assets, because they meet their monthly obligations from the income derived from investments.

What this kind of thinking and the resulting actions really does is move our possessions from one side of the ledger to the other. It moves them from the things we can't afford to the things we can afford. Doing without is a difficult habit to learn, but when we do learn it, our future will be much brighter.

> *The man who starts out with the idea*
> *of getting rich won't succeed. You*
> *must have a larger ambition. There is*
> *no mystery in business success. If you*
> *do each day's task successfully, stay*
> *faithfully within the natural operations*
> *of commercial law, and keep your head*
> *clear, you will come out all right.*
>   John D. Rockefeller

Giving

The Fallacy of Liberal Thinking

In our society today, especially in the area of politics, we often hear people referred to as liberals. Have you ever stopped to think about what the word 'liberal' really means when it's used in this context?

Since the early days of our nation's history, we have had labels for members of political parties. George Washington, for example, belonged to the Federalist party. Later on, Presidents Taylor and Fillmore belonged to the Whig party. Today, the two major political parties in our country are the Democratic and Republican parties.

In theory at least, each party represents a different political philosophy about how the government should serve the people. Within this context, we have given labels to people such as conservative, liberal and moderate. Each of these represents an attitude or philosophy a particular person holds in terms of how much government should do for its people.

In today's times, we identify liberals as people who want to do more and give more to the people they serve. Contrast this with the attitude of those identified as moderate or conservative who say our government has gone far beyond what it should be doing and it should conserve or cut back on the services it's now providing.

Which view would you take—liberal or conservative? Do you think our government should do more for the people or less? You might say 'more' which would certainly place you with the majority. If your answer was indeed 'more,' you have just identified yourself as a liberal.

Without prejudging, let's look further for a moment. Today in the United States Congress, there are a number of so-called liberals who say we should not balance the budget on the backs of the poor and we should not cut programs or services for the needy. On the surface, that's a pretty good argument, and it's true, if you don't take this line of thinking any further.

Unfortunately, what the poor do not know or understand is that they are exchanging their pride, self-respect, financial security, and votes for a congressman who can vote for his own pay raise or tax exemption. When you increase taxes to pay for more services, it's not a good deal. Except maybe for our congressmen who have just given themselves a pay raise!

A liberal is someone who wants to give away something he or she didn't earn and that's the saddest part of all. It's the fallacy of liberal thinking. To say it very simply, it's easy to be liberal with someone else's money.

This liberal way of thinking and conducting our nation's business affairs has created a national debt of over twenty trillion dollars and still many say government is not doing enough. At this rate, how much more can we afford for government to do? If we are to ever again have sound economic prosperity in this country, we must return to the old principle of 'an honest day's work for an honest day's pay.' When we earn our income, it instills self-respect and pride and we know its true value.

I hope the next time you vote, you will consider what I've said here: a liberal is someone who wants to spend money he didn't earn! And that's the fallacy of it!

Those who expect to reap the blessings of freedom, must, like man, undergo the fatigue of supporting it.

Thomas Paine

Human Relations

Do You Act
or React?

*If you want to know a lot about a person's
character, watch how he or she acts. But
if you really want to know, watch how he
or she reacts, because this is the real test.
In these days of shades and pastels, it's the
best way on earth for you to see a person's
true colors.*

Some time ago, I ran across a terrific article
titled, "Do You Act or React?" and I want to share
it with you. As you read it, think about how you
would act or react in a similar situation.

Do You Act or React?

I walked with my friend, a Quaker, to the newsstand the other night, and he bought a paper, thanking the newsie politely. The newsie didn't even acknowledge it. "A sullen fellow, isn't he?" I commented.

"Oh, he's that way every night," shrugged my friend.

"Then why do you continue to be so polite to him?" I asked.

"Why not," said my friend, "Why should I let him decide how I am going to act?"

As I thought about this incident later, it occurred to me the most important word was *act*. My friend *acts* toward people; most of us *react* to them. He has a sense of inner balance which is lacking in most of us. He knows who he is, what he stands for, and how he should behave. He refuses to return incivility for incivility, because then he would no longer be in command of his own conduct.

When we are enjoined in the Bible to return good for evil, we look upon this as a moral injunction, which it is. But it is also a psychological prescription for emotional health. Nobody is unhappier than the perpetual reactor. His center of emotional gravity is not rooted within himself where it belongs, but in the world outside himself. His spiritual temperature is always being raised or lowered by the social climate around him, and he is a mere creature at the mercy of these elements. Praise gives him a feeling of euphoria, which is false, because it does not last and it does not come from self-approval. Criticism depresses him more than it should, because it confirms his own secretly shaky opinion of himself. Snubs hurt him, and the merest suspicion of unpopularity in any quarter rouses him to bitterness.

A serenity of spirit cannot be achieved until we become the masters of our own actions and attitudes. To let another person determine whether we should be rude or gracious, elated or depressed, is to relinquish control over our personalities, which is ultimately all we possess. The only true possession is self-possession.

As I thought about this article, I realized just how much this affects us every day of our lives. It's not too difficult for most of us to act nicely, especially if we had the proper training when we were growing up. But it's just human nature to react to others in a negative way when they are rude, thoughtless or ungrateful toward us.

The Apostle Paul gave us the answer to this problem in Romans 12:2, "And do not be conformed to this world, but be transformed by the renewing of your mind, that you may prove what the will of God is, that which is good and acceptable and perfect."

The key to improving our human relations is to renew our thinking each day with good, honest and positive thoughts until it becomes a habit. Then when someone is rude or thoughtless, we will act toward them in a manner in our own best interests.

> *If we could read the secret history of our enemies, we should find in each man's life sorrow and suffering enough to disarm all hostility.*
> Henry Wadsworth Longfellow

> *Happy is the man that findeth wisdom, and the man that getteth understanding.*
> Proverbs 3:13

You Can Say It Without Putting People Down

Several years ago, I had a neighbor who had a beautiful white dog. Unfortunately, when the dog was let outside, he had a habit of visiting other neighbor's yards, bushes and flower beds, if you know what I mean.

One day, another neighbor whose yard had been visited by the dog made a comment about the dog's owner. She said, "I think I will give her a piece of my mind."

When the dog's owner heard about it, she responded, "If she gave it all, you still wouldn't have anything."

While it's natural to respond to criticism in this manner, it's much harder to stop and consider whether the other person's criticism is justified. No one who lives in the city, where houses are close together, wants to have to watch where they step in their own yard, especially if they don't own a pet and the problem persists.

The problem here as it relates to good human relations is that it's much easier to put someone down than it is to raise ourselves up. Unfortunately, because of the attitude of one neighbor and the resulting 'put down,' both neighbors were losers and they missed the opportunity to be friends.

I believe a lot of people are being misled today and here's an example. Some time ago, I was in a very large city in another state and I was listening to the radio. The program I was listening to during the noon hour featured a well-known psychologist who took calls from listeners who were having stress and emotional problems. After listening to the problem for a few minutes, the psychologist gave advice on how to cope with it. As I continued to listen, I am convinced that most of the listeners were satisfied with the answers because it was obvious the psychologist was well-qualified and knew what she was talking about.

Because of my extensive interaction with people, I picked up several things in the psychologist's answers that told me where she was coming from. First, her tone of voice was harsh, not soft and gentle, and the feeling of love toward others did not come through. Next, she seemed to be elated when some of her callers (especially female callers) asserted they were going to do something for themselves for a change, because they had been involved in taking care of others too long.

Before you misconstrue what I am saying, let me be quick to add, there is certainly nothing wrong with wanting to be our own person, to have self-respect, and a certain degree of independence, but there is a real danger in not knowing where to stop. In many cases, people who become assertive go from driving a motorbike to a Sherman tank if they are not careful. Before long, they develop the attitude that they can bulldoze their way over everything and everyone who gets in their way. This type of person has very little compassion for others.

People who are only interested in themselves and their rights are really Humanists. Regardless of whether by design or letting their selfish human nature take over, it's a shallow, short-sighted way to think and live.

I believe the people who put stock in the kind of information the psychologist was putting out are being misled. Sooner or later, regardless of what we say, or the lifestyle we choose, we have to come face to face with our Maker. We would be much better off if we would strive to always lift people up. In most cases, we can say what we need to say without putting other people down.

If you want to be miserable, think about yourself, about what you want, what you like, what respect people want to pay you, and what people think of you.

Charles Kingsley

It is not sufficient to know what one ought to say, but one must also know how to say it.

Aristotle

Make Sure You Are Worth More Than You Are Paid

Former President James A. Garfield once said, "Poverty is uncomfortable, as I can testify; but nine times out of ten, the best thing that can happen to a young man is to be tossed overboard and compelled to sink or swim for himself." The American free enterprise system offers tremendous opportunity for the individual who is always worth more than he or she is being paid.

Over the past several years, the term 'energy crisis' has become a reality in American society and it's causing many of us to change our habits. Whether it's a crisis or not, we know one thing for certain—the bills for energy-related products keep going up. In relation to utility bills, I remember several years ago when I used to get up each morning and turn up the thermostat to make our home warm and comfortable. As I said, our habits are changing. Now I get up and build a fire in the Franklin stove.

Let me ask you this question: Have you ever heard of someone going up to a cold wood-burning stove and saying "give me some heat, and then I will put in the wood?" Well, just for the fun of it, one day I tried it and I can tell you truthfully, it doesn't work! That stove just sat there and didn't do a thing! Finally, I gave up and put in some wood, stuffed some newspapers under the wood and lit the paper with a match. It wasn't long before it got so hot, I had to move my chair back.

My point is simple. I could have stood there and shivered for days and that stove would never have put out any heat. That is, not until I finally put in some wood and started it burning. I have just described a principle holding many people back on their jobs and keeping them from earning the amount of money they need and would like to have. While it's a little more complicated than this, it stems from the attitude many people hold that they would like to have the benefits *before* they produce or prove themselves to be worthy of the salary they started with in the beginning. In other words, they're saying, "let me start out with a high salary, then I'll prove I'm worth that salary."

Unless you are self-employed, too young or retired, please consider this: when a person is looking for a job and someone agrees to hire him, regardless of the starting salary, the employer is taking a chance the person is going to be worth at least what he is paid. If the employer is in the private sector, where a profit must be earned to stay in business, this means just breaking even. On the other hand, if the employee is worth more than he is paid, the difference is profit, and this is where future raises and fringe benefits come from.

If you are being paid eight dollars per hour, your value to your employer should be worth at least ten dollars per hour, because that's the only way you can have a financial future with the company. Take my word for it, if your employer is not earning a profit, there is no way he can pay you more money. Now he may pay you for a while, based on the value of other employees who are worth more, but it cannot and will not continue for long.

The next time you want to see this principle clearly, visualize that cold Franklin stove sitting there and me begging it for heat. If you really want to move up in your company and earn a lot more money in the process, the surest and most dependable way to do it, is to always be worth more than you are paid. To hold this attitude is the best financial security on earth.

> *The man who starts out with the notion*
> *that the world owes him a living*
> *generally finds the world pays its debt in*
> *the penitentiary or the poorhouse.*
>   William Graham Sumner

> *Everything comes to him who hustles*
> *while he waits.*
>   Thomas Edison

Friends

Are You a 'Fair-Weather' Friend?

*The late Dale Carnegie, founder of the
internationally famous course on public
speaking and human relations, once said,
"You can make more friends in two months
by becoming interested in other people than
you can in two years by trying to get other
people interested in you."*

I want to talk with you about friends. It has
been said we all need friends and I personally know
this is true. While some people may be considered
loners or recluses, in my heart, I believe they are
missing one of the greatest blessings in life. We all

need friends and even more importantly, friends need us.

How many friends do you have? Stop and think about this question. Do you have even one really true friend? That is, someone you can count on if you really need help and someone you know for certain would not let you down? I have several true friends I believe I can count on. However, we don't really know until that time comes, do we?

It has been my experience over the past several years that when I've needed help, I've had many people whom I thought were friends desert me. On the other hand, I've had other people, whom I didn't know were my friends, right there when I needed them the most. Have you also found this to be true in your life?

A conversation I had some time back brought these thoughts to mind. One day I was having lunch with my wife at the Arkansas Children's Hospital in Little Rock and I met a woman named Mildred Ward. Somehow, we got to talking about friends and she told me about a woman she knows who complained about not having any friends. Mildred went on to tell me why this was true.

One morning about two a.m., the woman's telephone rang and on the other end was an elderly woman who had fallen in her home and couldn't get up. So, she had called her friend (at least someone she thought was her friend), and asked her to come to her house and help her. Do you think she went? Well, the answer is no. It was too far. At least that's what she told her.

When the woman complained to Mildred about not having any friends, Mildred said, "I told her to her face, the reason you don't have any friends is because you don't know how to be a friend. You are a 'fair-weather' friend."

When you think about it, this is so true. Most of us can be a friend as long as the sun is shining and it doesn't cost us anything, but when friendship begins to cost us something, it has a way of setting the record straight. At this point the truth comes out and we are either a true friend or a fair-weather friend.

I received a phone call from a woman a while back who was not even a close friend. She said, "Bill and I have had an accident; can you come get us?" She told me where they were.

At this point, I didn't ask any questions, I said, "I will be there as quickly as I can get there."

The point I'm trying to make is simply this: if you want to have some true friends, be there when someone who calls you friend really and truly needs you.

He's the kind of friend you can depend
on, always there when he needs you.
Author unknown

Goals

How to Stay Out of a Rut

Did you hear about John Jones? He died some time ago and they inscribed these words on his tombstone: "Here lies John Jones. Died at age twenty-one; buried at age sixty-one." John Jones had been in a rut for forty years of his life.

Are you in a rut? In case this word isn't in your working vocabulary, I'm referring to the mental state many people fall into when they have performed routine, humdrum activities for so long, they have lost their zest for living. For the person in a rut, life is no longer exciting and rewarding.

Because it happens so slowly and over an extended period of time, most people who fall into a rut never realize they are in one.

I think most adults will admit falling into a mental rut at one time or another in different areas of life. This topic is very important because medical studies have shown boredom, a side effect of being in a rut, is a disease more crippling to the human species than most of us realize. The problems of boredom are manifold in our work force, schools, marriages, churches and anywhere else our thinking processes settle down into a well-worn groove.

If you are aware of the problems associated with boredom, have you ever asked yourself why people become bored? While the problem itself may not be easy to solve, the answer is simple. Whenever you find boredom, people in a rut, you will find the absence of a goal or a great motivating idea.

In my work with our nation's public schools over the past twenty years, I believe I have found part of the reason why people let themselves fall into a rut. While I'm sure the reasons are different for different people, basically it goes back to a person's education and habitual way of thinking. As I've conducted seminars with students in our schools, I've discovered something important in relation to communication skills. When you ask students to identify what is produced when you link words together, they will say *sentences.* When you take it one step further and ask what is produced when you link sentences together, they will say *paragraphs.* But the reason many people fall into a mental rut is because the world does not run on paragraphs.

The world runs on good ideas and unfortunately, most schools do not teach students to set goals or look for the ideas in a paragraph that will help serve other people. The only way we can succeed is to find a need and fill it. This requires us to constantly search for new and better ideas.

Going back to my earlier statement, when a person is bored, it is simply the absence of a goal or a great motivating idea. Unless we are taught to think along these lines, it's easy to become bored and fall into a rut. The truth is, we don't make exciting plans while we are in a rut. If we aren't careful, the best things in life will just pass us by.

Time, with all its celerity, moves slowly to him whose whole employment is to watch its flight.

Samuel Johnson

Nothing great was ever achieved without enthusiasm.

Ralph Waldo Emerson

Higher Than a Kite On Sunday, Lower Than a Snake on Monday

A woman went into the post office to buy stamps to mail her daughter's wedding invitations. "I'd like to buy two hundred stamps please," she said to the clerk." "What denomination?" he asked. "Oh, dear!" she said, "I didn't know it had come to that. I supposed it would be best if I split them. Give me one hundred Baptist and one hundred Presbyterian."

Have you ever known or been around someone who was higher than a kite on Sunday

142

but lower than a snake on Monday? I'm referring to those people who faithfully attend church every Sunday, but come Monday morning, you would never know they were the same people. Unfortunately, many people who are church members and call themselves Christian have never had a born-again experience where Jesus Christ came into their heart to live and to control their attitudes and actions. Without this personal encounter with the Lord, there is really no change inside.

It's possible for a person to put on their finest clothes, go to church on Sunday, sing and pray, but on Monday, it's just business as usual. The reason I know this is true is because it's the way I lived for most of my life. Robert Louis Stevenson once said, "When Christ came into my life, I came about like a well-handled ship."

Laying aside the spiritual aspect of our lives for a moment, let me point out that when we get serious about accomplishing anything worthwhile and begin to develop plans to achieve it, there are natural laws and principles that control everything in the world around us. The Law of Success, for example, is a two-edged sword. Operate on the right side of this law and it works for us; operate on the wrong side and it works against us. This law is also known as the Law of Cause and Effect and it literally controls everything in the universe.

Jim Davidson

People who are higher than a kite on Sunday and lower than a snake on Monday may not truly understand this universal law is actually working against them in their jobs for the rest of the week. What the rest of the world sees in these people is something we call 'double standards' and it not only hurts their witness for the Lord, it lets other people around them know the true nature of their character. No wonder people outside the church are skeptical of what they see and hear.

When it comes to double standards, not only the church is affected. Many parents live by double standards where their children are concerned. We have some wonderful teachers in our schools, but many unfortunately do not set good examples in terms of fostering the right kind of values in our young people.

You may say it's all a matter of what values you believe are important and this is certainly true. I'll settle for truth, honesty, decency (and that by Biblical standards), hard work, fairness, justice and respect for the rights and property of others. We need Christians and others in these permissive times to be committed to the things that count, not just on Sunday but on Monday, as well.

More things are wrought by prayer than this world dreams.

Alfred Lord Tennyson

Character

Permanent Change in our Nature —It's Not Easy

It is often said, "The measure of a man's real character is what he would do if he knew he would never be found out." Here, you name the crime or the sin, but whatever it is, our greatest temptation comes when we think we can commit it, and no one else will ever know.

One time I heard a cute story about a man who worked for a lumber yard that will illustrate this truth in a very compelling way. The man had worked for a lumber yard for over twenty-five years and during this period, whenever he needed some lumber for a project at home or to help a friend, he would just take it without paying for it.

Before I finish this story, let me remind you there are a lot of people who do this. Employee theft is one reason prices in today's times are so high because companies have to build in an extra profit margin to cover losses that occur this way.

Back to the story. One night, during a revival service at his church, the man was saved, and shortly thereafter his conscience began to bother him. He said to himself, "Oh Lord, what am I going to do?" He knew if he confessed his sin to anyone in the church and the word ever got back to his employer, he could be prosecuted and might even wind up in jail. Again, he thought to himself, "Oh Lord, what on earth am I going to do?"

Then he remembered something he had read. The Catholic Church has a confessional booth where people can go and confess their sins to a priest and never be seen. Since there was a Catholic Church nearby, this seemed like the right thing to do, so he made the necessary arrangements.

When the time came, he went into the booth and confessed what he had done for all those years. After he had finished, he said to the priest, "Father, is that all there is to it?"

The priest said, "No, you can't get off quite that easy. Did you ever make a novena?"

The man said, "No, but if you've got the plans, I know where I can get the lumber."

Obviously, this is not a true story, but the central point of the story is clear. Permanent change in our nature is not easy. A person who is inwardly a crook is just waiting on another chance to steal.

In my humorous story, the man was saved; that is, he had a conversion experience that comes about when people place their hope and faith in Jesus Christ. When people are saved, however, it does not mean they no longer sin. It just means they have a way to become forgiven for their sins. The goal for new Christians is to seek a daily walk with God and ask Him to teach them a better way to live. The process takes some time.

In recent years, psychologists have determined people's attitudes and character values are established at a very early age. Because of this, a person can be highly educated, but have serious character flaws and still wind up in prison. Even this person can change.

Permanent change in our natures—it's not easy.

Everybody thinks of changing humanity
and nobody thinks of changing himself.
                                        Leo Tolstoy

147

Children

I Loved You Enough

The dictionary defines "love" as "an intense, affectionate concern for another person." Love is the strongest of all human emotions and it was placed in each of us by a loving God, as a way to express our appreciation and commitment to those people and things that mean the most to us.

When we truly love someone, it is only natural to have that person's best interests at heart. There is no greater love in all the world than the love parents have for their children. This is a God-like instinct that is not only present in humans, it is also present in the animal kingdom. We see examples of this on every hand, and one that comes to mind is a very vivid picture I remember of a mother hen being burned to death in a fire and when she was removed, her baby chicks were still alive under her lifeless body. Now, as the song goes, "If that isn't love, I don't know what is."

While love is certainly the strongest emotion, it too, can get out of balance. We can love someone to the point our emotions tend to replace rational and logical thinking and as a result the actions we take can actually be counter-productive. Because most children are very perceptive, in some cases they actually use this strong love as an emotional tug-of-war to get their way, or to get what they want.

If you are a parent, grandparent, guardian, or someone else responsible for rearing a child, have you ever heard these words from your child: "You don't love me"?

Now, I'm sure in some cases the words, "You don't love me" are actually true. There are some people who never feel love and because of this, it's impossible for them to give love. However, in most cases the child who says, "You don't love me," is actually using these words as a tool to get what he or she wants.

In recent years, discipline has become a major problem in our nation's schools and also in millions of homes across America. If we are to reverse this trend, it is important for us to understand the difference between 'true' love and doing what is best for our children, as opposed to letting them use our emotions to do things that may not be in their best interests. It's my purpose to offer some positive suggestions and guidelines to help deal with the problem. In administering discipline and punishment to children, here are nine principles that should be observed.

1. Do not do it in anger.

2. Do not let discipline be in retaliation.

3. Do it in such a way as to not embarrass and humiliate the child.

4. Let the discipline be reasonable and let discipline be an expression of love.

5. Above all, ask God to give you divine wisdom in raising that child.

6. Keep your cool. Kids need the confidence that only a steady hand and a settled soul can offer.

7. Show your child that you are wise enough and strong enough to be the boss.

8. Be honest with your children. Tell them the truth.

9. Be generous with praise and when it comes time to criticize, your child will believe you and respect your judgment.

Raising children in today's times is not easy. There are so many pressures and problems in existence today that were not around fifty to one hundred years ago. But children are a blessing and they are a gift from God.

If we do a good job of raising them, when they are old enough to understand, we can say, "Do you remember when you used to tell me 'You don't love me'? Well, I loved you enough to ask where you were going, to make you clean your room, to not make excuses for your lack of respect and bad manners. I loved you enough to let you stumble, fall and fail, so that you could learn to stand alone. But most of all, I loved you enough to say 'no,' when you hated me for it. This, my child, was the hardest part of all."

> *Train up a child in the way that he should go, and when he is old, he shall not depart from it.*
>
> Proverbs 22:6

> *The work of a parent is nearly over when he loses his understanding for the young.*
>
> Author unknown

Business

Why It Pays
to Advertise

*It is often said that the American free
enterprise system is the eighth wonder of
the world and the average American's lack
of understanding about what it is, and why
it works, is the ninth wonder of the world. In
today's times of mass communication, many
of us are bewildered by the tremendous
number of advertising messages directed to
our attention on a day by day basis. Have
you ever stopped to consider where our
nation would be, if business people didn't
have the freedom to advertise the products
and services they produce?*

Just as most of the automobiles in the world today run on gasoline and must have oil or some type of lubricant to keep their internal parts from wearing out, marketing and advertising are the gasoline and oil that power the American free enterprise system. When new products and services are produced and are available for purchase, the only way the manufacturer can spread the word is through the medium of advertising.

To go one step further, consumers must know about products before they can purchase them. Purchasing generates profit which is the only way business can survive. It is the profit generated from the sale of products and services that provides salaries, fringe benefits, expansion capital, return on investment and the money for taxes to provide all public services in this country.

Most business people understand and accept the necessity of advertising, which is the primary reason we are inundated with advertising messages. The various ways a business can advertise its products and services are limitless, but there is an irony in the way most business people go about it. When business is good, they have the capital to advertise and they do, but when business is bad and capital is low, the first thing they cut back on is their advertising. The truth is, it should be the other way around. A business should spend most of its advertising budget when business is slow and cut back when business is good. Several months ago, I visited a woman at a radio station and she handed me a card titled, "Negative Thinking," and I want to share it with you.

Negative Thinking

A man lived by the side of the road and sold hamburgers. He was hard of hearing so he had no radio. He had trouble with his eyes, so he read no newspaper, but he sold good hamburgers. He advertised on radio, telling how good they were. He stood by the side of the road and cried, "Buy a hamburger, mister?" and people bought.

He increased his meat and roll orders. He bought a bigger stove to take care of his trade. His son came home from college to help him, but then something happened. His son said, "Father, haven't you been listening to what people are saying? If money stays tight, we are bound to have bad business. There may be a big recession coming on. You had better prepare for poor trade."

Whereupon the man thought, "Well, my son has been to college. He reads the papers, listens to the radio, and watches tv, and he ought to know." So, he cut down on his meat and roll orders. He cut down on his advertising and no longer bothered to stand on the highway to sell hamburgers, and his sales fell almost overnight.

"You're right, son," the father said to the boy. "We are certainly headed for a recession."

If you own or manage a business, keep the "Negative Thinking" article in the back of your mind the next time business is slow or economic predictions are not good. The surest way for our nation to go into a recession is for business people to stop advertising. Certainly, we can't spend all of our profit on advertising so we need to make certain our advertising is effective and reaching potential customers.

If you are a customer, keep in mind the prices you pay and the choices you have are due, in large part, to advertising. Without the medium of advertising, sales lag, profits fall off, and the American free enterprise system can no longer provide for the high standard of living most of us enjoy today.

The man who fails to advertise just because
conditions are a little uncertain is on par
with the farmer who refuses to feed his cows
because the price of butter has gone down.
E.T. Meredith Secretary of Agriculture
November 18, 1920

How to Shake Off
Negative Comments

You may be familiar with the saying, "Sticks and stones may break my bones, but words can never hurt me." This is one of the biggest untruths I have ever heard. We should never underestimate the power of words, because, if we let them, words can literally destroy our lives.

One of the best pieces of advice I've ever heard is to "live our lives so we wouldn't mind selling the family parrot to the town gossip." You can see the wisdom of this thought. While there is no way to control the negative things others may say about us, we should live our lives in such a way that no one would believe them.

While I never like to hear negative comments about me, those I love or the things I believe in, they do come along from time to time. When they do come, I can either shake them off and go on pursuing the goals important to me, or I can let them defeat me. The choice is mine.

Do you have trouble shaking off negative comments or negative things that happen to you? If you do, I believe the story I'm going to tell you will help you shake off negative comments in the future.

A farmer had a faithful old mule who had served him for years, but now it was becoming apparent with the passing of time, the old mule had just about reached the end of his days. As the farmer saw his old mule beginning to suffer, he realized he had to find a way to put him out of his misery. Being a kind, soft-hearted man, he couldn't stand the thought of just taking him out and shooting him, so he devised a plan.

Since the farmer was going to have to bury the mule anyway, he decided to lower him into an old, abandoned well and cover him with dirt. He thought this would 'kill two birds with one stone,' as the old well was a hazard and needed to be filled in. The farmer rigged up a tripod with a pulley and a hoist and lowered the mule into the well. While it was a sad day, the farmer thought it was the best way, so he got a shovel and a wheelbarrow and went to work.

As he poured load after load of dirt into the well, a strange thing began to happen. As the dirt fell on the old mule's back, he shook it off and tramped it down. This process went on for several hours, with each load of dirt being treated the same way. The old mule shook it off and tramped it down. Finally, the old well was completely filled in and the mule was standing on level ground. Then, he just walked away, free from the prison that was to be his grave.

This is not a true story, but it makes a wonderful point. The dirt thrown on the old mule's back could be compared to the negative comments and the negative experiences we all have from time to time. We can either shake them off, or let them bury us. The choice is ours.

I mentioned living our lives in such a way we wouldn't mind selling the family parrot to the town gossip. This is one of the best ways I know to keep from having too many negative comments said about us, but the next time it happens to you, I hope you will remember the story about the farmer and the old mule—just shake it off.

They sing. They hurt. They teach.
They sanctify. They were man's first,
immeasurable feat of magic. They
liberated us from ignorance and our
barbarous past.

Leo Rosten

Mama, I'm Sorry I Haven't Written Before Now, But...

How we view our circumstances in life is often a matter of perspective, and this is especially true when it comes to raising children. Here is an example of what I mean: "Our marriage would have broken up years ago if it hadn't been for the children," a woman said to a friend. "We can't get a divorce, because he won't take them and neither will I."

Children are a precious gift from God, but they don't always perform or act in a manner we would like for them to. As parents, we want the best for our children and in most cases have high expectations of them. Let me share a story with you to make my point. The story is about a college girl who wrote her mother the following letter:

Dear Mother,

I'm sorry I haven't written these last four months. The reason I haven't is because of a brain operation I had, which was the result of a concussion I received when I jumped from the fourth story of the dormitory when it caught on fire. Fortunately, a young service station attendant across the street saw the fire, called the fire department and the ambulance and got me to the hospital in time.

While I was in the hospital, the young man visited me regularly. When I was released, I had no place to go. He invited me to share his apartment. It wasn't really an apartment, it was just a basement room. It was kind of cute. Yes, Mother, I am in love. I'm pregnant, and we do plan to get married. The reason we haven't already gotten married is because of some silly disease he had and he failed the blood test.

Sincerely,
Your Loving Daughter

P.S. Now Mother, this is just to let you know, I did not have the brain operation. There was no concussion. I did not jump from the dormitory. It did not catch on fire. I am not in love. I'm sure not going to get married! I did make a D in English and an F in history. I thought you ought to see these two things in their proper perspective.

I believe you will agree, after the first part of the letter, the long-suffering mother was happy about a D in English and an F in history.

After reading this story, I began to reflect on it, and a couple of observations came to mind. Everything is relative, and only when we have the common sense to place things in perspective, are we able to properly deal with them. When you think about that daughter away at college (in all likelihood at her parents' expense), I'm sure her mother expected her to do better than a D in English and an F in history. The daughter knew her mother's expectations. Why else would she have gone to such great lengths to compose her masterpiece?

To profit from this story, let's consider the underlying fact that sooner or later we will be held accountable for our actions. This is true because in the final analysis we each have to live with ourselves, and if we shortchange ourselves in taking full advantage of life's opportunities, we are the ones who ultimately suffer the consequences. The message here is simple. Let's make sure we do our best to take advantage of our opportunities when we have the chance. Our success in life, in many ways, is like good human relations: "We only have one chance to make a good first impression."

Parenthood remains the greatest single preserve of the amateur.

Alvin Toffler

Little children, headache; big children, heartache.

Italian proverb

Persistence

The Slight Edge
—It Takes Only
Two Percent

The dictionary defines persistence as, "to hold firmly and steadfastly to some purpose or undertaking, despite obstacles." In reality, however, persistence is just another word for success.

Have you given much thought to the difference between the winners in life and the losers? Well, believe it or not, in most cases the difference is very little. In fact, it can be as little as two percent.

Some time ago, I read an article written by Gene Emmett Clark, D.D., titled "The Slight Edge—It Takes Only Two Percent," and I believe it will help you see what I mean. According to Dr. Clark, regardless of how well you have been doing, if you will do just a little bit more, it could mean the difference between winning or losing, success or failure, mediocrity or greatness.

The terms 'winning,' 'success' and 'greatness' are relative terms. Because one person is an outstanding success does not mean that someone else doing the same thing is a failure. Here is an example: When a touring professional golfer comes home to his local course, he would be considered great compared to the best players who play the course several times a week. This same golfer in the company of Jack Nicklaus, Gary Player, Arnold Palmer and Lee Trevino, would not be considered great. Keep in mind that winning, success and greatness are relative terms.

I believe Dr. Clark makes a good case in relating this principle to our own personal success. He begins by asking a question:

Have you been 'working like a horse'? I've been thinking about that expression, and at least one horse I can name has earned a pretty fair hourly rate. Someone figured up that the race horse Nashua earned more than a million dollars in a total racing time that added up to less than one hour. That's pretty good pay!!

Of course, we know that many, many hours went into preparation for that winning hour of racing, but here is something else that is important to understand. What makes this horse so valuable? You would probably pay a hundred times as much for a horse like Nashua, as you would just an ordinary race horse. But is this horse a hundred times faster? Of course not. What makes the difference in value is the fact that a horse of this caliber finishes just ahead of the rest, on a consistent basis. All he had to do was win a good share of the time by a nose to be worth a hundred times as much as an 'also ran.'

It's the same principle with human beings who are on top in the game of life. The difference between achievement and mediocrity is that extra two percent in study, application, interest, attention and effort. It is that one extra story for a writer, that one extra call for a salesman, that one extra putt for a golfer. In short, it's that little extra, that two percent, that often makes the difference between the winners and the losers.

Look around you. There are several ways to use this story to your advantage. What can you do to give it that extra two percent? If you will apply this simple principle in the areas of your life that really matter, it will bring you success out of proportion to the time and effort you will have to devote to it.

> *The whole idea is to somehow get an edge. Sometimes it takes just a little extra something to get that edge, but you have to have it.*
>
> Don F. Shula

Attitude is a Reflection of the Self-image

Have you ever wondered why some people have a negative, pessimistic attitude about most things while others are generally positive and up-beat? The answer, while very simple, is not really understood by the majority of people. Since they don't understand it, they don't know how to go about changing a negative attitude to a positive attitude, and in the process, living a more successful and productive life.

The reason one person is positive while another is negative is because attitudes or outlooks on life are a reflection of self-image. The discovery of the self-image has been called the most important psychological discovery of this century. Because this discovery has been in more recent times, many people did not learn about it in school or later in life as they moved out into the world.

Almost by chance, Dr. Maxwell Maltz, a plastic surgeon, discovered the concept of self-image, and later wrote about it in his book titled *Psychocybernetics* that has sold in excess of fifteen million copies. As Dr. Maltz worked with his patients to change their physical appearances with the aid of plastic surgery, he began to notice a corresponding change in their personalities. When his patients came to him, they were reserved and shy, but after surgery he noticed a definite, marked change in their willingness to tackle jobs and assume risks that would have been considered impossible before.

Further research revealed outward physical change was also accompanied by an inner emotional change. Thus, the conclusion was reached; the self-image is the mental picture we hold of ourselves, and this mental picture relates to both the 'outer' and 'inner' person and it literally controls our lives. When an individual holds a positive picture of himself, he performs better than when he holds a negative picture. This is the basis for the terms we use in society today to label people winners or losers.

We see evidence of poor self-image when a person will not look another person straight in the eye, or when introduced will not give his name, or if he does, it's the last name only. People with good self-images, the people we call winners, are like magnets. They attract success and this results in a positive attitude, while people with poor self-images attract those influences, people and circumstances that lead to failure. People failing in life have a negative attitude. Attitude is a reflection of the self-image.

How can you change or improve your self-image? The most important thing to realize is that you have real worth and value as a person. We are each unique and created in the image of God, and because of this, we have all the value and worth we will ever have when we are born. On the other hand, the value and worth we acquire as it relates to society and to other people, is what we do and how we use what we have been given.

You may be familiar with the story of the "Bar of Iron." A small bar of iron is worth about $5.00 to start with. Made into horseshoes, this same bar of iron is worth about $10.50. Made into screwdrivers, it could be worth $250.00; made into needles, it could be worth about $3,250.00;

and finally, made into balance springs for watches, this same bar of iron could be worth as much as $250,000.00.

This same thing is also true for another kind of material—you! Your value is determined by what you make of yourself. You can change your life for the better by changing your self-image, which is simply the way you see yourself, both physically and emotionally; that is to say, from both the outside and the inside. It also becomes easier to help other people when you understand the reasons behind their negative attitudes. Set about the task of finding good things about others and give them positive reinforcement as a basis to change the way they see or view themselves. We've done a great thing for another person when we can help them see the winner God created them to be. In reality, the more we help others, the more we help ourselves.

A happy smile on your face is the light in your window that lets others know you are home.

Dennis Waitley

Memory

Should You Go First

It's been said there are only two things for certain in this life—death and taxes. While death is a certainty for each of us, in many cases it is a traumatic experience for those who are separated from their loved ones. Because of this, it is vital that we find comfort in these times of our greatest need.

Each week in our Sunday newspaper there is a section featuring couples celebrating wedding anniversaries commemorating lengthy terms of marriage—some as many as sixty years and even more. Now, it goes without saying, for a couple to celebrate sixty years of marriage, they either had to get married very young, or they had to live to be very old. With the current divorce rate in our nation around fifty percent, these people are fast becoming an endangered species. There is something beautiful about a couple who have been able to stay together through thick and thin for many years.

In the vast majority of cases, one marriage partner lives longer than the other and this leaves one partner alone, save for family and friends, but sometimes they are all alone. One of the greatest problems today among the elderly is loneliness. I ran across a beautiful poem titled "Should You Go First," and I believe it will bring comfort to you or someone you love. The author of this poem is unknown to me.

Should You Go First

Should you go first, and I remain, to walk
  the road alone;
I'll live in memory's garden dear, with happy
  days we have known.
In spring I'll wait for roses red, when fades
  the lilac blue.
In early fall when brown leaves call, I'll catch
  a glimpse of you.
Should you go first and I remain, to finish with
  the scroll;

No lengthening shadows shall creep in, to
    make this life seem droll.
We've known so much happiness dear, we've
    known our cup of joy;
And memory is one gift of God, that death
    cannot destroy.
Should you go first, and I remain, for battles to
    be fought;
Each thing you have touched along the way,
    will be a hallowed spot.
I'll hear your voice, I'll see your smile, though
    blindly I may grope.
The memory of your helping hand, will buoy
    me on with hope.
Should you go first, and I remain, one thing I'd
    have to do.
Walk slowly down the path of death, for one
    day, I'll follow you.
I'll want to know each step you take, that I
    may walk the same.
For someday down that lonely road, you'll
    hear me call your name.

Some time ago I sent this poem to a friend
and she wrote back in less than a month to say a
favorite aunt had passed away and she was going
to share this poem with her uncle when the time
was right. If you are a young person you may not

be able to relate to this poem unless you have just lost someone close to you. Sometimes words have a special way of bringing comfort to our hearts. In every trial we face we need to know God loves us and someone cares. My prayer is that this poem will bring comfort to you in your times of need.

Make my joy complete by being of the same mind, maintaining the same love, united in spirit, intent on one purpose.

Philippians 2:2

Blessed are those who mourn, for they shall be comforters.

Ray Allen

The Seven Stages of a Marriage Cold

"Marriage is a deal in which a man gives away half of his groceries in order to get the other half cooked." While there may be some truth in this humorous definition, the institution of marriage is very important to the success of our nation, and a good marriage is worth working for.

If you are a married person, or planning to get married, I believe you will enjoy this little story I discovered some time ago. It's titled, "The Seven Stages of a Marriage Cold." This story has been around for some time and I'm not sure where it came from originally, but it illustrates the fact that in most cases, the happy, blissful state of marriage goes downhill as time passes.

While it certainly doesn't have to be this way, and there are exceptions to the rule, the first few days, weeks and even months of marriage are usually very happy times. Unfortunately, like many things where the new wears off, there is less enthusiasm and excitement for it. This dilemma can be seen through this story titled, "The Seven Stages of a Marriage Cold." Each stage represents one more year of marriage, by the way the wife's cold is handled by her husband.

Seven Stages of a Marriage Cold

First year: The husband says, "Sugar Dumpling, I'm worried about my baby girl. You've got a bad sniffle and I'm putting you in the hospital for a general check-up and a good rest. I know the food is lousy, but I'll have your meals brought in from the deli. I've already got it arranged."

Second year: "Listen Darling, I don't like the sound of your cough. I've called Dr. Miller to rush over here. Now, go to bed like a good girl, please, just for your dear old papa."

Third year: "Honey, maybe you had better lie down. Nothing like a little rest when you feel puny. I'll bring you something to eat. Do we have any soup in the house?"

Fourth year: "Look Dear, be sensible! After you feed the kids and get all the dishes washed, maybe you'd better hit the sack for a while."

Fifth year: "Why don't you get up and get yourself an aspirin? And stop complaining so much!"

Sixth year: "If you would gargle or something, instead of sitting around and barking in my face like a seal, I would appreciate it!"

Seventh year: "For Pete's sake, stop sneezing! What are you trying to do? Give me pneumonia?"

If you are a married person, I hope you have one of the happiest marriages to be found anywhere, whether you have been married for three days or fifty years. Marriage is one of the most basic of all institutions in our society. When marriages fail, we all lose, because it affects the family and America is a land of families.

Let's keep in mind a successful marriage is built on mutual trust, love and a lifetime commitment to each other. I believe someone said it best with these words: "Marriage is not looking at each other, it is looking in the same direction together."

> *Marriage is an arrangement instituted by God himself for the purpose of preventing promiscuous intercourse of the sexes, for promoting domestic felicity, and for securing the maintenance and security of children.*

Noah Webster

Contentment

The Worst Guilt of All

*There is a little five-letter word called guilt
that most people suffer from at one time
or another, and if it's not dealt with and
handled properly, the consequences can be
devastating.*

Unfortunately, many people go through
life carrying such a heavy load of guilt, they are
not free to develop and use their unique talents and
abilities. While guilt comes to each of us in a variety of ways, there is one special guilt I believe is
the worst guilt of all.

To begin, let us consider what British
statesman and author, Edmund Burke, had to say.

"Guilt is never a rational thing; it distorts all the faculties of the human mind, it perverts them, it leaves a man no longer in the free use of his reason, it puts him into confusion." Because we are unique, guilt affects each of us differently.

The primary reason guilt is so difficult to deal with is because complete freedom or release from guilt often involves soul searching and a confession or at least admitting our shortcomings. To confess or admit we are wrong goes against basic human nature and this is especially true for the person who has a poor self-image.

Let me ask a couple of very pertinent questions. What's inside a guilty person that causes him to feel this way? Are we born with a mechanism that tells us, or is it a skill or attribute we have to develop? Personally, I think it's both. We are each born with a conscience, which has been defined as "the faculty by which distinctions are made between moral right and wrong, especially in regard to one's own conduct." In other words, because we are each born with a conscience, we therefore have the inherent or built-in capacity to know whether what we do is right or wrong. It's how we use this built-in faculty that has a lot to do with whether we feel guilty or not.

Our conscience, figuratively speaking, can be compared to a triangle inside our hearts. When we do something we know is wrong, the triangle turns and the corners prick our hearts and it hurts. This is where the saying, "the pangs of our conscience" comes from. When we continue to commit acts we know are wrong, the triangle keeps turning and before long the edges are worn smooth and it no longer hurts. At this point, it is often said, "he has no conscience." This isn't true; the person still has a conscience, but it's become so dull from misuse that it no longer makes him feel guilty.

If we are to live happy, successful and well-adjusted lives, we should feel guilty when we lie, steal, cheat, or commit crimes against an individual or society. Otherwise, we will be totally insensitive to the needs of the people around us. The power of guilt is evident when we see people who have committed serious crimes and they feel such guilt for what they have done, they actually want to be punished.

It's very important for us to deal with the day-to-day problems and decisions that are the source of much of our guilt; however, there is a deeper and much more serious root problem that brings about the worst guilt of all. This is the awareness, deep in the innermost parts of our beings, that God has given us tremendous talents and abilities He wants us to develop and use to serve Him and our fellow man. When we don't develop and use what

He has given us, it creates a void. As a result, we experience a form of deep-seated guilt that gnaws at us regardless of where we go or what we do. There is only one solution to this problem and that's to put our heart and soul into those activities that we deem worthy of our time. It's only when we do our best with what God has given us, that we feel good about ourselves.

> *For nothing reaches the heart but what is from the heart, or pierces the conscience but what comes from a living conscience.*
> William Penn

Excellence

Who Are the Gifted?

In today's times we often hear the statement, "he or she is a very gifted person," but have you ever thought about what this statement really means? In checking my dictionary, the word "gifted" is defined as one having or showing great natural ability or one who is talented. As it's used in this context, the word gifted is really a label that is used to identify a person as being a cut above the average or one who has made some important contribution.

The word "gifted" means what the dictionary says, but I want to discuss with you the way the word is used as a label, because it has the potential to do irrevocable harm to some people. This is especially true in the lives of many young people who are immature and do not know how to deal with it properly.

I will never forget an occasion several years ago when I was speaking to a class of sixth-grade students. The teacher singled out one little boy and said, "Johnny is a member of the gifted and talented program." This made Johnny feel very important, but I'm sure she didn't realize what it did to the rest of her students, especially those who were not in the gifted and talented program.

In recent years we have discovered and learned about the self-image and the tremendous power it has over our lives. We have also come to realize that one of the most powerful and damaging things we can do to others is to pin negative labels on them. In most cases, without even realizing it, when we refer to other people as idiots, dumb, stupid or morons, we have not only pinned labels on them, we have given them mental pictures of themselves that, sooner or later, they will begin to accept as true.

The reverse is also true. When we pin positive labels on people, such as brilliant, smart, intelligent and gifted, they begin to visualize themselves in a different light and form mental pictures that create potential for full use of their talents and abilities.

I did not use labels that have to do with a person's outward physical appearance, since a quick glance in the mirror is all it takes to prove or disprove whether this kind of label is valid.

In relation to the emphasis the education establishment is placing on identifying gifted and talented students, I personally believe this new focus has some merit, because we all know as technology continues to advance, we will need our very best minds to help us solve problems.

There is, however, a great danger in this new focus, as illustrated in an article titled, "Who Are the Gifted?" written by Wilbert Larson of Fort Collins, Colorado. Mr. Larson points out that Albert Einstein was four years old before he could speak and seven years old before he could read. Isaac Newton did poorly in grade school, Beethoven's music teacher once said of him, "as a composer, he is hopeless." When Thomas Edison was a boy, his teacher told him that he was "too stupid to learn anything." A newspaper editor fired Walt Disney because he had "no good ideas." Caruso's music teacher told him, "You can't sing! You have no voice at all." Leo Tolstoy, author of War and Peace, flunked out of college. Abraham Lincoln entered the Black Hawk War as a captain and came out as a private!! Fred Waring was once rejected from high school chorus and Winston Churchill failed the sixth grade.

If we know seeming failures turned out to be world famous, how many others could have been if someone had not pinned a label on them or destroyed their confidence by ridicule? Yes, labels are very powerful and we need to be careful. When we look at any person, young or old, we just never know who are the gifted.

Talents are best nurtured in solitude;
character is best formed in the stormy
billows of the world.

Goethe

Faith

Who Should Read the Bible?

Prussian born Immanuel Kant (1724-1804), considered by many to be the foremost philosopher of the modern period, once said: "The Bible is the greatest benefit which the human race has ever experienced." To have the Bible and yet not read it, would be like going without food for several days, showing up at a banquet and saying, "I'm not hungry."

For some, the discovery of the eternal truths contained in the Bible comes early in life, for others, it comes much later. Some people never make this discovery, and as a result, they miss the benefits of knowing the God of the Bible in a personal way. As I look back over my own life, one of my biggest regrets is that I did not discover what was really in the Bible until a good portion of the race had already been run.

About five years ago, after agreeing to teach a boys' Sunday school class, I made the decision to read the Bible through once each year and I am fulfilling that commitment. Until I asked the Holy Spirit to guide and control my thinking and my life, I never dreamed the Bible was so rich and so exciting! Because I'm so excited about the Bible, I just wanted to share this with you.

In relation to this personal experience, I ran across something the other day titled, "Who Should Read the Bible?" I felt that it might be of value to you. Please give these words some thought:

Who should read the Bible? The young: to learn how to live. The old: to know humility. The rich: for compassion. The poor: for comfort. The dreamer: for enchantment. The practical: for counsel. The weak: for strength. The strong: for direction. The haughty: for warning. The humble: for exaltation. The troubled: for peace. The weary: for rest. The sinner: for salvation. The doubting: for assurance. All Christians: for guidance.

When I read this the first time, I came to the conclusion that it pretty well covers the waterfront.

It talked about the young, the old, the ignorant, the learned, the rich, the poor, the dreamer, the practical, the weak, the strong, the haughty, the humble, the troubled, the weary, the sinner and all Christians. Surely, you can see yourself in there somewhere. I know I can, several times. I'll confess to you that I'm a sinner and I need the Bible and its wisdom and encouragement each day of my life. You know, for people to be saved, they must first admit they are lost. My friend, whether you read the Bible or not, there is a good reason why this book is the all-time best seller. It contains truth, inspiration and guidance that can give our lives meaning, purpose and hope that no other source can give. I stand in awe of its power.

Now, I'm not a preacher, but just as someone who cares about others, I want you to know that God loves you and you are very precious to Him. That's what it says in the Bible.

Unless we form the habit of going to the Bible in bright moments as well as in trouble, we cannot fully respond to its consolations because we lack equilibrium between light and darkness.

Helen Keller

Honesty

Some Straight Talk
that Paid Off

*The Golden Rule is to "do unto others as
you would have them do unto you." But
there is another golden rule that also affects
the lives of many people. This could be
called the Economic Golden Rule, and it
can be summed up with these words: "He
who has the gold makes the rule." If we
don't also understand this other golden rule,
life can be very frustrating.*

One of the greatest blessings I have in
writing and producing a daily radio program is that
I get to meet and know so many fine people. This

personal contact with people in all areas of society is the primary source for the good ideas I collect and pass on. However, I realize a good idea in itself is of little value unless I can show you how to use it and how to turn it into a benefit for your own life.

Some time ago, I was sitting in the office of a friend, the owner of a funeral service with several locations in southern Mississippi. He told me a true story involving one of his employees that contains a very important principle.

It seems the mother of an employee had died recently and the employee was fast becoming an alcoholic. Word was beginning to spread that he was talking 'smart' to some of the other employees. Well, the problem reached the point that it became necessary for my friend to call him into his office. When he did, he closed the door behind him. After they chatted a moment, my friend looked him straight in the eye and called his name. He said, "You know your mother would not be proud of you and the way you are acting. You have a choice. You can either make your mother proud of you, or you can become a drunk. But you are not going to be a drunk and work for me." My friend went on to say, "I don't want your answer now. I want to give you a few days to think about it. But come Monday, you come in sober and be ready to work, or be ready to leave."

Well, that was almost ten years ago, and the man is still there and has become an excellent employee. He later told his boss, "Mr. ___, I ain't never had anyone talk to me like that."

With my friend, it was not just an employee with a problem, it was a human being he cared about. The lack of personal concern and caring is why many management people fail when it comes to dealing with employees who have personal problems. In many cases they treat them impersonally, yet wonder why their turnover rate is so high.

Another amusing part of the story about my friend's wayward employee is when still another employee was having a problem and the man told him, "You'd better straighten up. You don't want to go into the boss's office, and have him close the door behind you." There is no doubt about it, my friend had made a believer out of him!

In bringing this story to a close, there are several obvious things we can learn from this experience. Sometimes it's hard to find another person who cares enough about us to look us straight in the eye and tell us the truth. The truth may hurt, but in most cases, it's better to hear it and do something about it than go on living with the problem.

Of course, the primary reason the employee's problem was solved was because the 'economic golden rule' came into play. Sometimes it takes the thought of losing our jobs for us to change our attitudes and our behavior.

> *The improvement of the understanding is for two ends; first, for our own increase of knowledge; secondly, to enable us to deliver and make out that knowledge to others.*
>
> John Locke

Ideals

The Optimist Creed

*Did you hear about the man who went down
to the courthouse to see if his marriage
license had expired? This man was really
and truly an optimist, wouldn't you say?*

Over the years as I've done research for
many radio programs and countless speeches, I've
run across literally hundreds of definitions and
clever sayings for and about the word optimist. The
true optimist is someone who looks on the bright
side of things and searches for the beauty and good
in what happens to them each day. This positive
way of thinking and living soon develops into a
mental attitude that enables this type of person to

overcome the adversity and pitfalls we all encounter from time to time.

This positive mind-set or outlook on life is often referred to as optimism and is the basis for a service club called Optimist International. This organization, with headquarters in St. Louis, Missouri, is comprised of over three thousand clubs in the United States, Canada and Mexico.

Their motto is "Friend of Youth," and they make a great contribution to the development of our nation's young people, as well as those in other countries. The clubs that make up Optimist International meet each week, and during the meeting club members quote something called "The Optimist Creed." As a former member, I would like to share it with you. As you read the words to this creed, I encourage you to think about the possibilities for your own life. This I know for sure—there are times in my life when this positive and optimistic way of thinking is desperately needed.

The Optimist Creed

Promise Yourself:
To be so strong that nothing can disturb your
    peace of mind.
To talk health, happiness and prosperity to
    every person you meet.

To make all of your friends feel they are
  valuable individuals.
To look on the sunny side of everything and
  make your optimism come true.
To think only of the best, to work only for the
  best, and expect only the best.
To be just as enthusiastic about the success of
  others as you are about your own.
To forget the mistakes of the past and press on
  to greater achievements for the future.
To wear a cheerful countenance at all times
  and give every living creature you meet a
  smile.
To give so much time to the improvement of
  yourself that you have no time to criticize
  others.
To be too large for worry, too noble for anger,
  too strong for fear, and too happy to permit
  the presence of trouble.

I'll confess, in the past, before inflation and
many of our other national problems came along, it
was a lot easier to do these things. This is why I believe
the message in the Optimist Creed is so appropriate for
today. We all need to be reminded of these principles
and truths on a regular basis, because it's so easy to lose
sight of what our country is all about, and to realize just
how blessed we are as a people.

My point is this: we don't do our best when we feel discouraged. The next time you are feeling a little down, discouraged or blue, I hope you will remember the Optimist Creed. Just get it out and read it. I promise you it will help!

Because you have occasional low spells
of despondence, don't despair. The sun
has a sinking spell every night, but rises
again all right the next morning.

Henry Van Dyke

Education

Teach Kids to Say Yes Sir, No Sir, Please, Thank You, and You're Welcome

We've all heard some person make the comment, "I want to give my child a head start in the world." There is no better way to prepare a young person for success in life than to teach them respect for authority, to respect the rights and property of others, and above all, the importance of good manners, because all other educational experience will pale in comparison.

For over twenty years I've worked with our nation's public schools as a business consultant, and during this time I spent many hours attempting to motivate students and teach them about the American free enterprise system. As I began each session, I could always tell which students had received discipline and moral training at home and which ones had not. I have found the most accurate barometer for making a determination of this kind is a child's manners.

If they responded to my questions or in other forms of interaction with the simple words, "yes, sir," "no, sir," "please," "thank you," and "you're welcome," I knew without a doubt, they were willing and eager to learn. On the other hand, in a few situations where I was not shown the courtesy and respect that should have been afforded any guest, I knew some valuable time would be wasted as I had to first prepare them to learn. Students in settings of this type seldom, if ever, used the words, "yes, sir," "no, sir," "please," "thank you" and "you're welcome."

Unfortunately, this is the same problem that confronts many of our nation's school teachers. The fine young people who receive discipline and are taught good manners at home, are much easier to teach than those who are not. Unruly and disruptive students are stealing a valuable opportunity from those who want to learn.

After many years of experience, I'm convinced you can't teach children the really worthwhile things in life, if you don't first have their respect. In the case of administrators and school teachers, it usually goes back to their own childhoods. If they were taught manners and to respect other people, there is a good chance others will respect them. To say it another way, "we will seldom be placed in a position of authority, until we are first willing to submit to authority."

I'm really talking about leadership here, and there is only one word that will cover it—example. Regardless of what we say, our personal examples are what it will eventually come around to. To illustrate what I'm saying, please let me share this true story with you.

For several years I had been calling on a particular school superintendent, attempting to sell him my services, but he would never purchase any of my materials or even let me talk with his teachers and then he went on to tell me why. This public school in a town of about 1,500 people had just had their Junior-Senior Awards Program and it was conducted entirely by students. He said the program was a real disaster. The bad language, dirty jokes and the way these students conducted themselves was embarrassing and humiliating to the administrators and the teachers.

As he said, "It was a good thing the school board and the parents were not there." This situation had finally shocked him into realizing something had to be done. Well, it should have been done a long time before, starting at home by parents teaching these young people some respect, good manners and some old-fashioned discipline, but when they arrived at this school, they still needed leadership by example by both administrators and teachers.

Many schools have discipline; students are taught respect and you would never hear bad language or dirty jokes in any school program. In the case of the superintendent I mentioned, it all comes back to his own childhood. If you have never thought about it before and have children or grandchildren of your own, I would like to suggest for your consideration, if you want to give them a head start in life, teach them to say, "yes, sir," "no, sir," "please," "thank you" and "you're welcome." It will be great for them and it will be good for America.

Self-respect is at the bottom of all good manners. They are the expression of discipline, of good will, of respect for other people's rights and comforts and feelings.
Edward S. Martin

Children

The Meanest Mother
in the World

*Have you ever run across someone who was
just plain mean? "Mean" in this sense is
the adjective form which refers to someone
lacking elevating human qualities such as
kindness and good will. Mean people are
unkind, maybe even to the point of physical
harm, and it's obvious they do not care
about other people. However, people's
motives for their actions really determine
whether they are mean or not. On the
surface people may appear to be mean,
when in reality, they are not mean at all.*

To illustrate the truth of what I'm saying, I want to share an article with you that I picked up at our local printer. It's titled "The Meanest Mother in the World," and no author is listed. I am happy to say my mother has many of the same qualities. If you have children or grandchildren, please think about what this article is saying and what it could mean to you personally.

The Meanest Mother in the World

As a child, I had the meanest mother in the world. She was real mean. When other kids ate candy for breakfast, she made me eat cereal, eggs and toast. When other kids had coke and candy for lunch, I had to eat a sandwich. As you can guess, my dinner, too, was different from other kids. My mother insisted on knowing where we were at all times. You'd think we were on a chain gang. She had to know who our friends were, and what we were doing. She insisted that if we said we would be gone for an hour, that we would be gone for one hour or less.

She was real mean. I was ashamed to admit it, but she actually had the nerve to break the child labor laws! She made us work! We had to wash the dishes, make all the beds, learn to cook and all sorts of cruel things. I believe she lay awake at night thinking up mean things for us to do. She always insisted on telling the truth, the whole truth and nothing but the truth. By the time we were teenagers, she was much wiser, and our life became even more unbearable. None of this tooting the horn of a car for us to come running. She embarrassed us to no end by making our dates come to the front door to get us. I forgot to mention, while my friends were dating at the mature age of twelve or thirteen, my old-fashioned mother refused to let me date until I was fifteen or sixteen.

Boy! Was she mean. My mother was a complete failure as a mother. None of us have ever been arrested, or beaten by a mate. Each of my brothers served his time in the service of his country—willingly, no protesting. And, whom do we have to blame for the way we turned out? You're right! Our mean mother. Look at all the things we missed. We never got to take part in a riot, never burned draft cards, or got to do a million and one things our friends did. Our mean mother made us grow up into God-fearing, educated, honest adults. Using this as a background, I am trying to raise my children.

I stand a little taller and I am filled with pride when my children call me 'mean.' You see, I thank God that he gave me the meanest mother in the world.

To my way of thinking, this article, "The Meanest Mother in the World," contains many worthwhile values to live by and to raise our children by. In today's times some people may call us old-fashioned, but that should not concern us if what we are doing is right and best for those we love.

The most important thought I ever had
was that of my individual responsibility
to God.

Daniel Webster

Responsibility

You Can't Sink Half a Ship

The legendary football coach Vince Lombardi once said, "No one ever fails in life, until he blames someone else." Unfortunately, many people in our prosperous nation were never taught that accepting responsibility for themselves and their actions is the most visible sign of maturity. This is a personal quality that will contribute greatly to individual success, and it's also a vital need if we are to preserve our freedom in the perilous times in which we live.

I want to ask you to create this scene in your mind. Just before the break of dawn one cold winter morning, a family is standing out in the street in their pajamas watching their home burn to the ground. As they huddle together and hear the distant sound of the fire truck on its way to the fire, they begin to think about the loss of their most cherished possessions, many of which can never be replaced. But at this moment they are thankful just to be alive.

Now, as we all know, this scene actually takes place thousands of times each year in America and many families are not as fortunate as those I've just described, as their lives are lost in the tragedy of a home fire. There are also many of our nation's firemen who perish in the line of duty. However, for those who are fortunate enough to escape with their lives, they can start over and rebuild. In a few years, in most cases, their lives can be back to normal.

Now what I've just shared with you is a parallel to graphically illustrate that everything is relative. We don't appreciate fair weather until we have suffered through several weeks of rain or snow. Most of us don't appreciate good health until we have had an accident or prolonged illness of some kind. Most Americans won't appreciate freedom until they come face to face with the distinct possibility of losing it.

One time I heard the late Dr. Ken McFarland, noted speaker, author and guest lecturer for General Motors, tell the story about the first mate of a ship who rushed up to the captain and said, "Sir, the ship is sinking!" to which the captain calmly replied, "Let her go, she ain't ours." Dr. McFarland then went on to make a very important point. He said, "If we are on a ship, it is ours, regardless of who owns it." You see, when a ship goes down, every person who is on it, goes down with it.

You know, one of the greatest gifts God has given us is a mind with unlimited potential and powers most of us never use. Accepting full responsibility for yourself and your actions can make a real difference in our nation's future. There is a good chance you already conduct your affairs in this manner, and if this is the case, share with those around you just how important it is.

The reasons are many, but the United States of America is sailing through some tough economic seas just now, and we have many social problems begging for a solution. If we are to maintain our precious freedom, American citizens need to accept responsibility for themselves and their actions and we must believe it's possible. This principle also applies to our homes, our jobs and careers and especially how we treat those around us. To show love, kindness and concern for others is also a sign of maturity. To remember what I've said, just keep this thought in the back of your mind: you can't sink half a ship. The whole ship stays up, or the whole ship goes down, and it is yours, if you are on it.

> *Many times a day I realize how much my own outer and inner life is built upon the labors of my fellow men, both living and dead, and how earnestly I must exert myself in order to give in return as much as I have received.*
>
> Albert Einstein

> *Great responsibility must go hand in hand with great privileges.*
>
> Theodore Roosevelt

Marriage

Ten Rules for a Happy Marriage

When it comes to the importance of marriage, I believe Benjamin Franklin said it best: "A single man is not nearly the value he would have been in a state of union. He is an incomplete animal. He resembles the odd half of a pair of scissors."

Marriage is an institution ordained of God and it has been the desired standard for two adults living together in an intimate relationship since the earliest days of our nation's history. While there are millions of people in our nation today who are married, unfortunately many of these people are not happy in the marriage relationship. While this is a very complex issue, unhappiness is the primary reason the divorce rate is now around fifty percent, which means that about half of all new marriages will only last one to three years. This has placed a tremendous strain on the American family and the home, which is the foundation of our society.

In my view, one of the greatest problems associated with marriage is the misconception that a good marriage is supposed to be happy all the time. While true happiness should be the goal of every marriage, it's not realistic to enter into marriage with the belief this will always be the case. You see, marriage is much more than the idea of achieving happiness. It must be based on a total commitment by each partner that they are going to make the marriage work and they will stay together through the good times and the bad times.

Now, if you or someone you know has the need, I believe I have an idea to share with you that will help. As I've counseled people over the years, I've found most of the problems that arise between husband and wife come after the honeymoon is over. As it relates to marriage, the honeymoon is usually a trip or short period of time after the wedding when the couple can spend some time alone.

What some people may not realize is the greatest opportunities for a long and happy marriage can be found in the true meaning of the word honeymoon. Actually, the state of honeymoon, or that special feeling, time of grace, or whatever you want to call it, can last a week, month, year or a lifetime. You see, the secret to a happy marriage is to never let the honeymoon end. If you want to know when the honeymoon is over, it's when he no longer bothers to open the car door for her, and she no longer bothers to fix her face for him.

Someone has suggested "ten rules for a happy marriage" and I would like to share them with you. If you are in an unhappy marriage, or even if you are not, some of these suggestions or rules could make a real difference.

1. Never both be angry at the same time.

3. If one of you has to win an argument, let it be your mate.

4. Never yell at each other unless the house is on fire.

5. Never bring up mistakes of the past.

6. Neglect the whole world, rather than each other.

7. Never go to sleep with an argument unsettled.

8. At least once each day, try to say one kind or complimentary thing to your life's partner.

9. When you have done something wrong, be ready to admit it and ask for forgiveness.

10. It takes two to make a quarrel and the one in the wrong is the one who does most of the talking.

The greatest potential for good in these ten rules lies in the fact that anything becomes habit if it's repeated. If you will make a sincere effort to put these ten rules of a happy marriage into practice, it could easily result in a good marriage becoming even better and it could even save a marriage that is failing.

What joy! I have found the perfect mate.
He has a marvelous sense of humor,
enthusiasm for the future and a steadfast
faith in God. And, oh, yes! He loves me!
Velma Seawell Daniels

Courage

Do You Have the Courage to Say No?

To have courage in the face of adversity is one of the greatest of all human virtues. The late Winston Churchill, former prime minister of Great Britain, had this to say about courage: "It is the quality which guarantees all others."

As the topic of courage relates to your own life, here is a question I would like for you to think about. Do you want the best life has to offer? I'm confident most people will answer "yes" to this question. It's just human nature to want the best life has to offer. However, in many cases we settle for far less than it's possible for us to achieve.

The only way you can have the best life has to offer, is to learn how to say no at the right time and in the right way. Most of our obstacles to having and living the best life, are brought about when we don't have the courage or intestinal fortitude to say no.

Almost from the time we are born and come into the world, life is made up of one decision after another. For those of us who are fortunate enough to have had loving parents, to have received a good education, and to have made some positive choices, we began our journey through life with a lot going for us. Of course, for those who were not so lucky, there is always hope they will encounter enough positive influences to make a real difference.

Regardless of how comfortable the ride in reaching adulthood and individual responsibility, it's here our ability or courage to say no really comes into play. To make sure we are speaking the same language, allow me to go to the dictionary for the meaning of the word no. It means: "not so, as opposed to yes, and a term used in expressing refusal, denial or disagreement."

In your own life, can you think of problems that were created because you didn't have the courage to say no? I can. I can think of a thousand cases where I would have been better off if I would have just had the courage to say no. Here are some examples where the simple word no would make a big difference in a person's life.

No—to pre-marital sex.

No—to drugs.

No—to smoking.

No—to alcohol.

No—to profanity.

No—to crooked or unethical business practices.

No—to breaking the law.

No—to cheating on your mate.

No! No! No! It's a powerful word when it's used in the proper way and at the proper time. Now, as the author, please don't think for a moment that I'm setting myself up as a perfect example of someone who has had the courage to say no to each of these life changing decisions. In fact, there are only a few things on this list where I can truthfully say I've said no to in every case. Based on my years of experience, however, if I had the chance, knowing what I know now, to do it all over again, my list of things I would say no to would definitely be longer.

Decisions have to be made where we are, and in the circumstances we find ourselves. This is why we need to make these kinds of decisions in advance, so when we are confronted with a choice of this type, it will already be settled. I believe you will agree we do need a standard to live by, and something we can depend on to be right in every possible situation.

We hear a lot these days about positive thinking, and no is not a positive word, in fact, it's negative. That is one reason a lot of people don't like to even say the word. Also, when we say no in a group environment, it shuts off the fellowship, and who wants to be a wet blanket?

In most cases the lack of courage comes from fear. And the word fear, in this case, can be seen in the acrostic, "false evidence appearing real." In the vast majority of cases, we are afraid because we don't know enough or because we are acting on information that is untrue. When it comes to life changing and life altering decisions, I hope you will give some serious thought to what I've been saying. The courage to say no is the only way to have the best that life has to offer.

> *Last, but by no means least, courage—moral courage, the courage of one's convictions, the courage to see things through. The world is in a constant conspiracy against the brave. It's the age-old struggle: the roar of the crowd on the one hand and the voice of your conscience on the other.*
> General Douglas MacArthur

The Scars on the Door

Winston Churchill once said, "How little we can foresee the consequence either of wise or unwise action of virtue or of malice! Without this measureless and perpetual uncertainty, the drama of human life would be destroyed."

This quotation by Winston Churchill reminds me of the little boy who crawled under a big tent, thinking he was getting into the circus free, but when he got inside it turned out to be a revival meeting. Life is filled with surprises and disappointments of various kinds, but this is one facet of life which makes it so interesting. As

Winston Churchill said, much of the drama of life would be destroyed if this were not the case.

From my perspective, it would be wonderful if there was always something good, exciting and worthwhile waiting just around the next bend in the road or in the next day's mail or the next phone call, but we know this is not reality. Life is made up of good days and bad days, happiness and sorrow, and success and failure. Life is just this way.

We can, however, make personal choices to ensure the law of averages will work to our advantage to have more good days than bad days, more happiness than sorrow, and more success than failure. In other words, it's not what life does to us, it's what we do to life that counts. The reason this is true is because of the natural law that controls everything in the universe, called "cause and effect." If we take care of the causes, the effects will take care of themselves.

We read in the Bible in Galatians 6:7— "Be ye not deceived, God is not mocked, for whatsoever a man sows, that shall he also reap." Most people believe this and know it's true, but we do not always base our actions on this great truth. Rather, we permit other factors to influence our decisions and for the time being forget that sooner or later we will reap the consequences of our actions.

Because we are creatures of habit, we just continue to think and act in a certain vein until our habits are changed by some outside force. Since most of our important values and habits were established when we were young, I felt the following story might be of value to you.

It seems a farmer had a rebellious son. This youngster was forever getting into trouble. Not serious trouble, just things that were out of character for the way he was raised. Finally, one day the father suggested to his son: "Son, every time you do something that you know is not right, I want you to take a hammer and drive a nail in the front door of our barn."

Every so often during the next few weeks, the father would hear the tat-tat-tat of the hammer as the son was driving nails in the barn door. This went on for several months, until the barn door was almost covered with nails.

At this time, the farmer made another suggestion. He said, "Son, now every time you do something that you know is right, I want you to pull a nail back out of the door." Well, the son took his suggestion and little by little the nails began to come back out of the door. To be sure, they didn't come out nearly as fast as they went in.

Finally, one day the nails were all out, and the son told the father, "Father, I see what you mean. I thought I would be happy when I got all the nails out, but I didn't realize all the scars that would be left on the door."

I hope you can see the point of this story. While outside influences can help us change our values, attitudes, and habits, in most cases the consequences of our actions will still be there. Everything we do in life has a consequence and there is always a price which must be paid. With this in mind, let's do our best to live the kind of life that will bring us the most happiness and the most success and in the process be a positive influence in the lives of others.

That which follows ever conforms to that which went before.
                                    Marcus Aurelius

A cynic is a man who knows the price of everything, and the value of nothing.
                                    Oscar Wilde

The T. J. Miracle Diet

These days it seems like half of the country is on a diet and the other half is thinking about it. One of the best stories I've heard about a person being on a diet is about a salesman who was observed eating some very 'thin' soup. When someone asked him if he was on a diet, he said, "No, I'm on a commission."

A few weeks ago, I was visiting one of our radio sponsors, and I couldn't believe how much weight she had lost since the last time I had seen her. She said both she and her husband had lost a lot of weight and they were feeling great. You know, many of us go through life like we're carrying around a big rock everywhere we go, and that extra five, ten, twenty or even fifty pounds, keeps us from doing a lot of things that could be so much fun. Personally, I never had a problem with my weight until I was around thirty-five years of age, but ever since, I've been like a yo-yo—up and down. At the present time, I'm "hesitating," if you know what I mean.

If you have a problem with your weight, I have something to share with you that I believe will be of interest. It's a diet called the "T. J. Miracle Diet" my wife brought home one day, when she was employed by a local hospital. As a general rule, I don't put too much stock in these so-called "miracle" diets, because they starve you to death and you usually gain all the weight back the minute you quit starving.

This "T. J. Miracle Diet," however, is based on the one and only sensible approach to losing weight. If you eat more calories than you burn, the rest of it is going to fat. It's as simple as that. In addition to losing weight, this plan will also help you flush your system of impurities and give you a feeling of well-being.

Here then, is the plan that will help you lose from ten to seventeen pounds and feel like a million dollars in only seven days.

T. J. Miracle Diet

Day One: All fruits except bananas. For melon lovers, this is just the day for you!

Day Two: All vegetables. Eat all the fresh or cooked vegetables of your choice. Try to eat "leafy" vegetables and stay away from vegetables such as dry beans, peas, and corn.

Day Three: Fruits and vegetables. Same as Day One and Two, except no potato.

Day Four: Banana and skim milk along with "T. J. Miracle" soup (this consists of onions, peppers, whole tomatoes, cabbage, celery and soup mix or seasoning). Incidentally, you may eat this soup as often and as much as you wish.

Day Five: Beef and tomatoes. You may have ten to twelve ounces of beef and six tomatoes on this day. Try to drink at least eight glasses of water to wash away the uric acid in the body.

Day Six: Beef and vegetables. Eat all the beef and vegetables you want, but no potato.

Day Seven: Brown rice, fruit juice (unsweetened) and vegetables.

While this diet only lasts seven days, obviously you could repeat it as often as you felt the need, depending on your desired weight. When you take a moment to examine this diet, it's so easy to see why it works. The nutrition is there but the calories are not. Remember—to lose weight, you simply must burn more calories than you are taking in.

> *"Going on a diet is a system of starving yourself to death so you can live a little longer."*
>
> Jan Murray

Perspective

You Tell Me
I'm Getting Old

It's often been said that "Age is mind over matter; if you don't mind, it doesn't matter." There is a great deal of truth in the saying, "You're only as old as you feel." To feel good most of the time is a blessing that many of us take for granted.

When it comes to the subject of old age, someone once said, "Old age is a club that with luck we all join." I'm looking forward to it, aren't you? You may respond by saying, "I'm already old." This may be true in a chronological sense, because I know many who will read this book are elderly people. Did you notice how I switched terms? There is a vast difference in being elderly and being old. That is to say, we get old when it comes to our thinking and our ideas, which is another way of saying we are not very progressive.

What prompted these thoughts is a poem I ran across the other day titled, "You Tell Me I'm Getting Old." While reading this poem, I discovered it contained a profound message and I would like to share it with you. It's my sincere hope it will be a source of great encouragement for you.

You Tell Me I'm Getting Old

You tell me I'm getting old. I tell you that's not so!
The house I live in is worn out, and that of course, I know.
It's been in use a long, long while; it's weathered many a gale;
I'm really not surprised you think it's getting somewhat frail.
The color's changing on the roof, the window's getting dim.
The walls a bit transparent and looking rather thin.
The foundation not so steady as once it used to be.

My house is getting shaky, but my house isn't
    me.
My few short years can't make me old.
I feel in my youth, eternity lies ahead, a life of
    joy and truth.
I'm going to live forever there; life will go on,
    it's grand.
You tell me I'm getting old, you just don't
    understand.
The dweller in my little house is young and
    bright and happy;
Just starting on a life to last throughout eternal
    day.
You only see the outside, which is all that most
    folks see.
You tell me I'm getting old, you've mixed my
    house with me.

Dora Johnson

The message this poem contains is very clear. For Dora Johnson and those of us who have experienced the free gift of eternal salvation made possible through the blood of the Lord Jesus Christ, life will go on for eternity. While this is a very personal decision and this is between you and your God, I care about you and where you will spend eternity.

In reality, every book must have a final chapter, just as every person's life will someday come to an end. To me, it would be tragic to pursue our goals in life and strive to become a success and then get to the final chapter only to discover that we had missed the whole point of life. Whether you are a religious person or not, physical death is something that sooner or later we all must face.

Finish each day and be done with it.
You have done what you could. Some
blunders and absurdities no doubt crept
in; forget them as soon as you can.
Tomorrow is a new day; begin it well
and serenely and with too high a spirit
to be cumbered with your old nonsense.
The day is all that is good and fair. It is
too dear with its hopes and invitations to
waste a moment on yesteryears.

Ralph Waldo Emerson

Subject Index

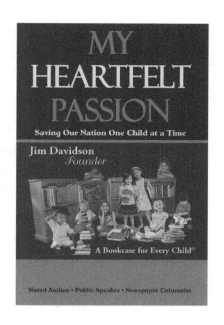

Dear Fellow American,

If you love being involved in community projects, the book *My Heartfelt Passion: Saving Our Nation One Child at a Time* will provide you with an opportunity, and supply all the details to begin a unique literacy project called "A Bookcase for Every Child." In 2005, a committee of like-minded citizens founded this project in my hometown of Conway, Arkansas. We provide a personalized oak bookcase and a starter set of books to pre-school children being reared in low-income families. Statistics say these children have few, if any, books to read before entering school and are the most likely to drop-out and cause massive problems later in life, impacting all of society.

Up to this time, we have given 750 of these bookcases to Head Start children and over 2,000 nationwide, as we have projects in six states. The child who grows up in our society without learning to read does not have a prayer when it comes to achieving success. We have had over 5,000 people involved in our project, in one phase or another, as we hold an annual Bookcase Literacy Banquet in October to raise the funds to build the bookcases and then hold an annual Awards Ceremony to present the bookcases and books to our children in April, before the end of the school year.

We have had great success with this project and have made a tremendous difference in the lives of some very special children. This is an all-volunteer "giving back" community project and no one earns a penny for their good work. This project helps us to live out this old saying: "The success of any community comes when citizens plant trees whose shade they will never sit in." Available at: www.amazon.com, www.barnesandnoble.com and www.sbprabooks.com/JimDavidson

God bless,
Jim

Review Requested:
If you loved this book, would you please provide a review at Amazon.com?

CPSIA information can be obtained
at www.ICGtesting.com
Printed in the USA
BVHW081753090919
557952BV00014B/1787/P